PRO WRESTLING IN MEMPHIS

PRO WRESTLING IN MEMPHIS

A HISTORY

G. WAYNE DOWDY

Published by The History Press
An imprint of Arcadia Publishing
Charleston, SC
www.historypress.com

All images courtesy of the Memphis and Shelby County Room, Memphis Public Libraries.

First published 2025

Manufactured in the United States

ISBN 9781467159920

Library of Congress Control Number: 2025935719

CONTENTS

PREFACE

In the year 2000, I attended a book signing at Burke's Bookstore for the author Pete Daniel, who had recently published *Lost Revolutions: The South in the 1950s*. When I walked in, a friend of mine introduced me to a giant of a man whose steel-like hand enveloped my own. At first, I didn't realize who he was, but then it hit me: *This is Sputnik Monroe!* I had heard of this man all my life—his ferociousness in the wrestling ring, his embrace of Black people and his antics on the streets of Memphis. I was a bit dumbstruck, but he was very kind, and we had a wonderful conversation. Thirty years before, my grandfather William Nance severely cut his finger at work, and while waiting in the emergency room to be stitched up, in walked Sputnik. He put his hand on my grandfather's shoulder and said, "Oh, I'd be out of business if I cut my hand like that." This is Memphis. No matter where you turn, you're likely to run right smack into professional wrestling. For a century, wrestling has reflected and influenced the culture of Memphis in ways small and large. It encompasses not only the kindness of Memphis but also its cruelty and violence. Because of this, it is the most important sport ever performed in the Bluff City.

Like most Memphians, I have been influenced by the mat game. I loved to watch the wild storylines that played out on Saturday morning TV. I remember watching the film from the infamous Tupelo Concession Stand Brawl, Jerry Lawler's classic insults, Jimmy Hart's ugly laugh and Lawler piledriving Andy Kaufman. I didn't necessarily keep up with every match, but I knew all the wrestlers' names because they were a part of the city's atmosphere. My brother Bud loved pro wrestling, and he often went to the Coliseum on Monday nights with our grandfather John Dowdy. Once Grandaddy became so enraged he grabbed Jimmy Hart's arm and had to be pulled away by Bud and a security guard. Professional wrestling is an authentic slice of Memphis life, and I hope this book will play a role in keeping it alive.

I dedicate this book to my uncles Larry and Ron Nance, as well as my beloved nieces and nephews: Britney Amber Dowdy Pierce, Larry Hank Pierce, Mallorie Ann Pierce, Cody Austin Dowdy, Farrah Dawn Dowdy, Lawton Ryan Dowdy, Lily Paige Dowdy, Evan Caruso and Brandon Ryan Dowdy.

I also wish to thank my colleagues in the History and Social Sciences Department at the Benjamin L. Hooks Central Library—Gina Cordell, Verjeana Hunt, Scott Lillard, Kyle Liotta, SeCoya McNeil, Bonnie Pinkston, Brett Prather, Laura Talley, Marilyn Umfrees and Cindy Wolff—for their friendship and encouragement. The History Press is a wonderful publisher to write for, and I thank everyone there for their support, especially Senior Acquisitions Editor Chad Road. And finally, I wish to thank Gina Cordell; Paul Gahn; my godson, Ellis Nelson Cordell Gahn; Derrick E. Patterson; and Peyton Dubose.

Chapter 1

"A FOOTHOLD IN MEMPHIS"

1894–1925

Personal violence has long been used in Memphis to settle disputes. In the 1850s, an enslaved person named Mary Herndon arrived in Memphis to be sold at Nathan Bedford Forrest's slave market. On her first day in the Bluff City, she witnessed "lots of white men, all drunk, some fightin' and some standin' about." Forty years later, Zach Claxton punched the pastor of Beale Street Baptist Church in the face, kicked him and bit off the end of one of his fingers. For decades, these rough-and-tumble versions of wrestling were sometimes employed in Memphis by brutal men seeking satisfaction in the Bluff City's muddy streets. However, it was not until 1894 that a demonstration of professional wrestling took place in Memphis. In September, German athlete Professor Fred Roeber arrived in the city to exhibit the sport of Greco-Roman wrestling. Despite its ancient-sounding name, this style of wrestling was developed during the mid-nineteenth century in France. Prohibiting any holds below the waist, Greco-Roman wrestling spread throughout Europe, where Roeber's brother Ernest was crowned champion. A match was held at the Pastime Athletic Club between the professor and Mike Carney, which the *Commercial Appeal* described as "a very scientific one and pleased the spectators immensely."

Two months later, the Pastimes Club began adding wrestling matches to its regular boxing exhibitions. The first contest took place on November 6, where two hundred spectators watched Carney wrestle a man named Dooley to a draw. For the next few years, small wrestling matches were held during larger boxing contests, but it did not become a very popular sport. Once the initial excitement died down, few people ventured out to see wrestling without having other athletic contests to view. For example, on October 25, 1897, a wrestling bout was scheduled at Germania Hall on Jefferson Street, but so few attended that the match had to be canceled.

Meanwhile, a different type of wrestling was spreading across the United States—containing elements of Irish collar-and-elbow, Japanese jiu-jitsu and the rough-and-tumble Lancashire, England style—known as catch-as-catch-can. According to historian Scott M. Beekman, "with holds below the waist allowed, unlike Greco-Roman, and victories obtained from falls and submission moves, catch proved to be a quick, violent, and exciting style." Exciting, yes, but many Americans first saw catch wrestling at carnivals and fairs, making it appear like a dirty sideshow rather than a professional sport. Memphians were first exposed to this type of wrestling in January 1901 when promoter and manager C.H. "Doc" Hottum secured a match between Lou Baptiste of St. Louis and Boston's Eddie Donnelly at the Phoenix Athletic Club. Fewer than one hundred spectators attended the match, which saw Baptiste employ a half nelson and crotch holds to defeat Donnelly.

Doc Hottum was perhaps the most colorful sportsman in Memphis history. Hottum moved to Memphis from Detroit in 1892 and soon distinguished himself as a local daredevil. He fractured his skull when he dived into the Wolf River and hit a metal piling. Doc's next stunt made him a local celebrity. The Frisco Bridge was then being built across the Mississippi River at Memphis. He jumped off the bridge and swam to shore, which delighted spectators. Once, Hottum fought five men outside the Shelby County Courthouse and later stopped a runaway horse team near the corner of Main Street and Monroe. Hottum promoted every kind of sport, including an annual swimming race in the Mississippi River, and managed several famous prizefighters, including John J. Sullivan, Jake Kilrain and Battling Nelson. His shrewd understanding of promotion convinced Hottum that wrestling had all the dramatic ingredients to become a popular sport.

As Hottum worked to bring catch wrestling to the Bluff City, it was bursting in popularity in many other parts of the United States. It was aided by the creation of two championship belts, the American and World Heavyweight titles, which were fought for by wrestlers across the country. As a result, the two most popular wrestlers in the country were Frank Gotch, who in 1904 defeated Tom Jenkins for the American Heavyweight wrestling belt, and world heavyweight champion George Hackenschmidt of England. On April 8, 1908, Gotch and Hackenschmidt met in Chicago for the first nationally recognized title bout in catch wrestling history. Gotch's victory over the champ made him America's first superstar wrestler and led to widespread interest in the sport. Writing of this famous bout, historian Ken Zimmerman Jr. concluded that "the first match between Frank Gotch and George Hackenschmidt made professional wrestling the most popular sport in America for three years."

Meanwhile, back in Memphis, Doc Hottum continued to book contests whenever he could. In 1907, two matches were held at the Hippo Rink, where Al Christensen defeated Jack Lewis, and the "Heavyweight Indian" War Eagle crushed Jim Parr at Germania Hall. One month after his victory over Parr, War Eagle fell to Frank Gotch in Chicago.

In January 1909, Wild Tom Coburn defeated Joe Acton, which gave him a shot at the American Middleweight championship, held by George Baptiste. The two grapplers met in Memphis a week later, where Baptiste employed a scissors hold to defeat his opponent. Two months after Baptiste secured his middleweight belt, Doc Hottum achieved his own triumph when he hired Gotch to perform in Memphis on April 29 against a young athlete named John Berg, who wrestled under the name of Charley Hackenschmidt. As soon as the announcement was made, Hottum was inundated for ticket requests, not only from Memphians but also from residents of Arkansas and Mississippi. The demand was so high that Hottum negotiated with the railroads to offer discount fares for those attending the match.

The night before the scheduled bout, heavy thunderstorms and high winds formed in eastern Arkansas that became a raging tornado as it passed into Memphis. The cyclone smashed into the Shelby County hamlets of Capleville and Whitehaven near the Mississippi border, killing 20 citizens and injuring 50. The storm continued its destructive path, killing at least 250 people in West Tennessee, North Mississippi and northern Alabama. This tragedy prevented many from going to the Gotch fight, but still 1,500 people attended the event. When the match began, Gotch warned Hackenschmidt to "look out for your foot," as the champ twisted his ankle and pinned him for the first of three falls. Seven minutes later, Gotch pinned young Hack with a head-and-bar hold, and three minutes after that, using the same hold, Gotch finished him off. Although popular, the Gotch bout did not lead to an increased demand for wrestling in the Bluff City. In fact, it would be nearly a year before wrestling returned to Memphis, when Emanuel Bruggilio met James Christy in March 1910.

Doc Hottum gave up on wrestling, but a few professional bouts were scheduled between 1911 and 1923. For example, the Gayety Theater offered a match between middleweight champion Joe Turner and John

Kilonis in February 1915. Bob Ackerman and the Masked Wrestler generated some heat in 1916, but it did not last long. It was not until 1923 that regularly scheduled wrestling matches returned to the city when boxing promoter Billy Haack began holding wrestling bouts in between prizefights. A great deal of opposition met Haack when he brought wrestling back to Memphis. Local sportswriter Herbert Caldwell was scathing in his criticism: "Wrestling and boxing won't mix. Memphis is a boxing town and has never taken enthusiastically to the mat game. It was given a thorough trial here about 10 or more years ago and went flat." Caldwell then warned that "if he continues to mix wrestling with boxing, Haack may unconsciously find himself in hot water."

Although he had abandoned wrestling a decade before, Doc Hottum never gave up on bringing quality professional grappling to Memphis. At the end of 1923, Hottum booked a rising star from Greece named Jim Londos for a bout at the Lyric Theater. Nicknamed the "Golden Greek," Londos was a stunningly handsome man who soon drew the lustful attention of the young women of Memphis. In his first match in the Bluff City, Londos was pummeled by his opponent Paul Schmidt, who employed armlocks, body scissors and toe holds for the first twenty-five minutes of the contest. Then when it appeared that the Golden Greek was on his last legs, he exploded on the mat with arm scissors and then used a double nelson with his legs to slam Schmidt to the canvas. Londos hammered Schmidt with a series of headlocks that disoriented him and led to his first fall. After a quick break, the two were at it again. Fifteen minutes after the bell rang, Londos used a scissors hold to push Schmidt to the mat and hold them there. Five hundred people attended the contest, which was described by the *Commercial Appeal* as "good, clean wrestling all the way through." Hottum's success pushed Billy Haack out, leaving Doc with control of the wrestling game.

Encouraged by the attendance and the positive press, Hottum partnered with St. Louis promoter John Contos to increase the number of wrestling bouts in Memphis. Contos had booked many wrestling matches in St. Louis, including a rematch between heavyweight champion Stanislaus Zbyszko and the former champ, Ed "Strangler" Lewis. More than six hundred people paid to enter the Lyric Theater on the evening of January 9, where they watched Jim Londos defeat Ivan Mikiloff, while Memphis firefighter Mike Meroney suffered two falls in a loss to the Bulgarian Boris Demitroff. Three weeks later, the partners brought former heavyweight champ Zbyszko to fight Londos in a bout that would determine who would meet the current champion, Ed "Strangler" Lewis. Zbyszko was guaranteed $2,000 regardless

In the 1920s, Jim Londos was the first "King of Memphis Wrestling."

of who won, and in turn, he promised to pin the Golden Greek in two falls within seventy-five minutes. He got his money but not the two falls. Londos avoided his traps and was able to defeat the aging ex-champion easily. Unfortunately for Londos, the Strangler refused to give him a title bout. He did, however, agree to wrestle in Memphis in a non-title fight with Demetrius Tofalos. Employing his famous headlock, the Strangler gave Tofalos his first fall after twenty-three minutes in the ring. Five minutes later, Lewis used a jiu-jitsu armlock to defeat Tofalos and collect a $1,500 fee.

Meanwhile, Londos continued to wrestle every month in Memphis. In February, he defeated jiu-jitsu champion Tarro Miyake, and in March, he crushed Joe Palmini. Then, out of the blue, the Strangler agreed to a non-title bout with Londos in St. Louis on April 2. It took Lewis more than an hour to get the Golden Greek in a headlock, which resulted in the first fall. Twenty-two minutes later, Londos employed a toe hold that felled the Strangler and forced him to hobble from the ring. When the contest resumed, Lewis threw Londos across the ring, knocking him unconscious. After waiting fifteen minutes for the Golden Greek to revive, the referee awarded the match to the Strangler. The following day, Londos took the train to Memphis, where he wrestled the Russian Ivan Lenow the following night. Still groggy from the previous night's concussion, Londos struggled in the beginning, which allowed Lenow to introduce a combination of head scissors, toe hold and wristlock that felled Londos twenty-nine minutes into the bout. The Russian lost the second fall when Londos employed a strong wristlock. Frustration took control of Lenow, who smashed his fist squarely in Londos's face. The referee immediately called a foul against the Russian and awarded the bout to Londos. In July, Londos met Renato Gardini at the Russwood Park baseball stadium in a match that ground on for three hours without a fall. When the timekeeper announced the three-hour mark, a police constable named Jacobi entered the ring and stopped the slugfest.

As 1924 ended, Jim Londos was the city's most important wrestler due to his victories over Andreas Castanos and Wladek Zbyszko in October and December. Throughout the year, matches had been well attended—according to sportswriter Mallory Chamberlin, "wrestling appears to have gained a foothold in Memphis by virtue of the square manner in which the show has been handled"—but that did not translate into financial success. There were still some who believed the sport to be a racket, and the Lyric Theater was not big enough for larger crowds to attend matches. Consequently, Doc Hottum retired from wrestling, leaving Contos the sole promoter in Memphis. He was able to land Strangler Lewis in January 1925 to wrestle again in Memphis, but the match was called off after Lewis sustained serious injury and lost his title to Wayne Munn.

At this point, Billy Haack again sought to promote wrestling along with his long-standing boxing contests. He was able to undercut Contos by signing new heavyweight champ Wayne Munn for a wrestling exhibition in Memphis with his partner Jack McCarthy. On the evening of March 17, the exhibition was about to get underway when Wladek Zbyszko stood up from his ringside seat and jumped into the ring. Peeling off his coat, Zbyszko demanded to take McCarthy's place. Haack entered the ring and ordered Zbyszko out. When he refused, Haack smashed Zbyszko in the face. Police officers and spectators rushed the ring, overpowered Zbyszko and threw him out of the squared circle. Just when order was restored, George Katsonaros demanded to wrestle Munn. Haack and the police roughed up the uninvited wrestler as they pushed him out of the ring. Both assailants were then escorted from the building, and the exhibition got underway. Haack later expressed his belief that a rival promoter had ordered Zbyszko and Katsonaros to disrupt his match. The logical suspect was John Contos, who denied involvement even though the two disruptors were scheduled to wrestle for Contos three nights later. Zbyszko, the brother of Stanislaus Zbyszko and the 1917 AWA heavyweight champion, explained that he had entered the ring to challenge Munn to a match but became excited by the crowd and forgot what he was doing. For the *Commercial Appeal*'s Herbert

Many early wrestling matches were held at the Lyric Theater.

Caldwell, the "disgraceful demonstration," sounded the "death knell…for the wrestling game in Memphis last night." Caldwell assumed that the three hundred fans who attended the match were as mortified as he was.

But they weren't. The next bout scheduled after the March 17 melee took place at the Lyric Theater on March 20, where the king of Memphis wrestling, Jim Londos, fought Katsonaros. Londos lost the first fall after Katsonaros used a half nelson and crotch hold but quickly came back with five flying headlocks to secure the second fall. Katsonaros tried to take the third fall with his own headlocks but could not overcome Londos's defense, allowing the Golden Greek to secure victory. One week later, Londos defeated "The Turk," Yussiff Hussane, in a match that was also well attended. Winning these bouts in front of large crowds not only secured Londos as the top grappler in the Bluff City but also proved that the death knell of wrestling had yet to be rung.

Chapter 2
"CLAMPED INTO A BODY SCISSORS"
1925–1930

By the spring of 1925, John Contos had created a stable of wrestlers who performed often in Memphis. These included not only Londos, Wladek Zbyszko and George Katsonaros but also Andreas Castanos, the Bulgarian Dan Koloff, Oresti Vidalfi and the "Gigantic German," Karl Steinborn. These matches, along with the occasional national title bout, secured wrestling's place in Memphis, but a whiff of carnival chicanery could still occasionally be smelled. In May, Contos brought heavyweight champion Stanislaus Zbyszko to grapple with Londos, Vidalfi and Boris Demitroff. Zbyszko vowed to throw each man twice within seventy-five minutes. The three challengers were supposed to enter the ring together and toss coins to determine what order they would wrestle. Expectations were soon dashed when it was announced that Demitroff would not wrestle, and the coin toss was canceled. The crowd mostly wanted to see Londos, but it was announced that Vidalfi would wrestle first. It took Zbyszko forty-five minutes to pin Vidalfi for the first fall. Many spectators walked out in disgust as the sweaty wrestlers tried to gain advantage over their opponent. Vidalfi threw a headlock on the champ, but he soon broke loose. Vidalfi then slammed Zbyszko to the mat and pinned him when the referee inexplicably stopped the match. It was then announced that Londos would not wrestle, and the event was over.

Herbert Caldwell, who called Zbyszko the "'sham-pion' of heavyweight grapplers," was livid, as were many in the crowd. The criticism was so effusive that Contos left Memphis and didn't return until four months later. On

Heavyweight champions Stanislaus Zbyszko and Ed "Strangler" Lewis wrestled many times in Memphis.

Friday, September 18, Contos held matches between Rudy Dusek of Little Rock, Arkansas, and Nebraska's Jimmy Hanson, along with a preliminary bout featuring Boris Demitroff versus Tony Devechi. Caldwell attended the event with an open mind and was impressed with what he saw. The Little Rock grappler use two flying mares and a headlock to defeat the Nebraskan in the first fall. In the second, Dusek repeated his moves to defeat Hanson in fifty minutes. Meanwhile, Demitroff easily finished off Devechi with a toe hold. Despite its success, this match was one of the last organized and promoted by John Contos. While he had been away, others were working to build their own wrestling territory, which was aided by the construction of the new twelve-thousand-seat municipal Auditorium.

At the end of September, Doc Hottum organized the first wrestling bouts in the new Auditorium. He brought Ed "Strangler" Lewis back to Memphis, where the former champion defeated Mike Romano, two falls out of three. John Contos continued to organize his own matches at the Lyric Theater. On October 20, Rudy Dusek defeated Chicago's Paul Martensen in two falls. In the second contest, Charlie Rentrop met the Italian Oresti Vidalfi in a match scheduled to last one hour. The two wrestlers employed armlocks and body scissors, but neither secured an advantage over the other. As the clock ticked down, the bout turned ugly, as both men slugged and gouged their opponent. When referee Mike Meroney clearly saw Rentrop gouge Vidalfi's eyes, he moved in to disqualify him. Realizing that he was about to be thrown out, Rentrop punched the ref in the chin, knocking him unconscious. Police swarmed the ring, and when Meroney woke up, he gave the match to Vidalfi. His victory over Rentrop provided Vidalfi with the chance to wrestle against the current heavyweight champion, Joe Stecher. The two met on October 28, and Stecher, using his body scissors hold, crushed the Italian in forty-three minutes. By the end of October, it looked as though Contos had finally overcome the effects of the Zbyszko incident. He confidently organized another wrestling card for November 6 but had to cancel when his headliner, Josef Rogacki, failed to show up to meet the popular Dick Daviscourt. This failure forced Lyric manager Vincent Carline to refund more than $400 in ticket sales.

Two weeks later, Contos organized another card, which included Daviscourt versus Jim Browning and Katsonaros taking on Bob Davis. When the first match began, Browning threw a headlock on Daviscourt that bloodied his nose. Daviscourt pulled out of the headlock and staggered toward the ropes. The match ground on for an hour without either man achieving a fall against his opponent. In the other match, Caldwell wrote that "Katsonaros won the first fall in 31 minutes. Up to that time Davis had much the better of the match. With Davis on the Greek's back and with his legs wrapped around the Greek, Katsonaros fell backward on Davis, knocking the breath out of him. Katsonaros quickly turned and flattened Davis on the canvas." Davis won the second fall, but Katsonaros then tripped Davis and pinned his shoulders, winning the decisive fall and the victory. In early December, Browning suffered another defeat when Jim Londos easily dispatched him with two falls in what was the final wrestling match held at the Lyric Theater. One last bout of 1925 was held on December 16 at the Southern Athletic Club's new Memphis Stadium. Daviscourt and Browning met for a rematch that soon turned ugly. The two men exchanged harsh words that led to angry blows. The crowd reveled in the violence and, according to Caldwell, "howled, stood on their seats and hollered." When the flushed audience left the arena, they had no idea that the Memphis wrestling landscape was soon to be changed forever.

John Contos, tired of the grind and disappointed in the high cost and low attendance, decided to quit the game. Moving to Atlanta, he hoped to bring high-quality wrestling to North Georgia. Back in Memphis, his place was taken by the wrestler and referee Charlie Rentrop, who received financial backing from a shadowy group of wealthy businessmen and support from the Memphis Athletic Club. Born in Hagen, Germany, Rentrop won the gold medal for middleweight wrestling at the 1904 Olympic Games in Athens. Four years later, he immigrated to the United States, where he frequently wrestled in several parts of the country. Moving to Memphis in 1929, Rentrop promoted matches and became the city's most important leader in professional wrestling. In his inaugural show at the municipal Auditorium on January 15, Rentrop presented Wladek Zbyszko versus the Wisconsin Giant George Hill, Rudy Dusek against Harry Mamos and the Masked Marvel against Carl Sampson. Rentrop's goal for solidifying Memphis wrestling under his control was to bring to the Bluff City as many national names as possible. Soon after his first event, Rentrop secured an appearance by the nation's reigning heavyweight champion, Joe Stecher. However, he ran into difficulty finding a grappler willing to fight the champ. After several unsuccessful inquiries, a Chicago wrestling promoter offered George Boganz, a 235-pound wrestler who was similar in build and strength to former heavyweight champion Stanislaus Zbyszko.

On January 27, the Auditorium was filled with anxious fans looking forward to championship-caliber wrestling. Stecher entered the ring first, and then a lanky, baby-faced wrestler weighing only 175 pounds and looking nothing like Stanislaus Zbyszko followed him. When the announcer identified the youthful grappler as George Boganz, whispers of surprise rippled through the audience. Sensing the fans' unease, the announcer apologized for Boganz's appearance, which was only the beginning of his humiliation. The champ toyed with the smaller Boganz for thirty-seven minutes until he dispatched the challenger with two quick falls. Fortunately for Rentrop, the second bout between the Masked Marvel and George McLeod fed the crowd what they wanted. The Marvel used body scissors and a reverse double armlock against McLeod for the first fall, and then the masked man employed nine consecutive headlocks on McLeod to throw him to the mat for the second and final fall. Despite the great action of the second match, Rentrop knew that he risked alienating fans because of the Boganz debacle.

However, no one really cared. By 1926, wrestling had become so ingrained in Memphis that it would take more than a scrawny grappler and a boring match to uproot it. With the Marvel's win over George McLeod and two other opponents, Memphians were intrigued by the masked wrestler and wondered who he really was. They didn't have long to wait. In February, the Marvel wrestled the "Bald Syrian" Frank Ojile. Between the two falls inflicted on the Syrian, the Marvel's mask was ripped off, revealing the face of Pete Sauer from Seattle. The following month, Sauer defeated John Ballas and, while

In 1926, world heavyweight champion Joe Stecher appeared in Memphis.

still flush with victory, challenged Jim Londos to a match after he destroyed the "Russian Cossack" Ivan Zarynoff. The two met at the Memphis Athletic Club's new indoor stadium, where they fought each other to a draw. Up to this point, Londos was considered by many to be the uncrowned king of Memphis wrestling. However, the crowd turned against him, jeering the Golden Greek while cheering for Sauer. In the hopes of reclaiming his popularity, Londos signed with Rentrop and the Memphis Athletic Club for ten bouts to be held throughout the rest of the year. He soon racked up victories against Zarynoff, Daviscourt and Joe Komar. With these victories, Londos met heavyweight champion Joe Stecher in Philadelphia, where Londos was defeated in one fall. He then spent the summer and early fall on the West Coast racking up victories he hoped would lead to the heavyweight championship.

As Londos's career suggests, Memphis was an important stop for contenders and national heavyweight champions to build support and retain their title. Joe Stecher returned to Memphis in the spring of 1926 to fight the Bulgarian heavyweight Nick Velcoff. No doubt embarrassed by his first visit to Memphis, Stecher put on quite a show for the local fans. Meanwhile, Rentrop was a far more successful promoter than his predecessor John Contos. In addition to securing financial assistance from local business leaders and receiving support from the Memphis Athletic Club, the signing of Londos to a long-term deal provided additional guarantees of success for Memphis wrestling. In the summer of 1926, he expanded his reach even further when he partnered with the American Legion to bring more wrestling bouts to Memphis. Dick Daviscourt, George Katsonaros, Tony Devecchi and George Actor all wrestled to popular acclaim, but grappling fans could not wait for Jim Londos to return to the Bluff City.

On November 4, their hopes were realized when Londos returned to Memphis. Performing at the Memphis Athletic Club's Stadium, the Golden Greek stood against the Italian Tony Devecchi. The fans screamed when

Devecchi used three flying headlocks to defeat Londos in the first fall. It looked bad for Londos when Devecchi employed punishing armlocks, headlocks and wristlocks. The Italian then leaped at Londos, who used his foot to force Devecchi to the mat. As the Italian rose, Londos slapped a strong headlock on him, threw him in the air and then pushed him hard into the mat. With Devecchi unconscious when he landed, the Golden Greek pinned him to the canvas and won the second fall. Fifteen minutes later, Devecchi had not regained consciousness, so the victory was given to Londos.

One month later, heavyweight champion Joe Stecher put his title on the line in a bout with the Lithuanian Joe Komar. Komar had recently won matches against Devecchi, Vidalfi and Jack Rooney and was seen by some as a possible heavyweight contender. However, he was very unpopular with Memphis fans because of his excessive roughness against smaller opponents. To build excitement and bring fans to the Stadium, Rentrop hired pioneering airplane pilot Vernon Omlie to drop thousands of handbills over the city, of which one hundred also contained free passes to the match. Stecher easily pinned Komar to the mat for the first fall, and during the required fifteen-minute rest period, a doctor examined Komar and found that he had a sprained back and could not continue. The audience was delighted that the Lithuanian had been busted up. Despite his loss, Komar was still seen as a contender for the heavyweight title, but he had to get through Londos first. The Golden Greek had little trouble with the belligerent Lithuanian when they met on January 13, 1927, at the Stadium. Five minutes after the bell, Londos trapped Komar in a Japanese wristlock for the first fall, and an hour later, he subdued the Lithuanian with three flying mares and a body straddle. In addition, Londos fought and defeated Tom Draak in two separate bouts, as well as crushing Rudy Dusek's younger brother, Ernie. Londos's victories not only further secured his place as the wrestling king of Memphis but also increased his chances of capturing the heavyweight title.

Another contender for the heavyweight belt was Rudy Dusek, the "Bohemian of Little Rock," who returned to Memphis in February to brawl with the "Terrible Turk" Yussiff Hussane. Dusek nearly defeated Joe Stecher in Little Rock, and he hoped, like Londos and Komar, that a Memphis match would bring him closer to the title. Hussane quickly fell from a well-placed side headlock for the first fall, and when the Bohemian used a grapevine and a reverse headlock, the Turk slid to the mat in defeat. A few weeks later, Dusek slammed the "Russian Ex-Cossack" Count Ivan Zarynoff in two falls and in March pinned Nick Velcoff to the mat. Meanwhile, another Memphis favorite, Dick Daviscourt, met Stecher in Philadelphia on May

20, 1927, where the champ used a head scissors hold to pin him to the mat. After his victory, Stecher agreed to put up his title in a rematch with Daviscourt in Memphis. The following week, a massive crowd jammed the Stadium arena to watch the heavyweight champ battle for his title. Thirty-four minutes into the bout, Stecher took down Daviscourt with a body scissors move. Six minutes later, Daviscourt caught the champ in a series of headlocks that helped him gain the second fall. Then Stecher, in the words of Herbert Caldwell, "secured a back standing body scissors. He worked Daviscourt to the mat, rolled him over and quickly had him clamped into a body scissors and his shoulders flat in three minutes." On January 26, 1928, Londos returned to Memphis, where he met the Nebraska wrestler Paul Jones. Throughout his career in the Bluff City, the Golden Greek had relied on defeating his opponent by wearing him down; then, in the last few minutes of the round, he would strike with a flying mare hold that usually brought victory. He tried this against Jones, but it didn't work. When the bell ended the match, no one was declared winner.

One of the impediments facing Charlie Rentrop in his bid to grow the wrestling business was having to shut down matches during the summer months because it was simply too hot in the Memphis Athletic Club's Stadium. This problem was solved when an outdoor arena was built at the Memphis Associated Amateurs Hodges athletic field. Two thousand fans attended the first matches held at the new arena on May 31, 1928. They watched as Paul Jones used his hooked body scissors move to defeat Joe Bruno and Toots Mondt roughly beat Jack McGuire in two falls with a combination crotch hold and body slam. By the late 1920s, there were several regional organizations and territories that offered heavyweight titles, although the American/World Championship first won by Frank Gotch in 1908 and subsequently held by Ed "Strangler" Lewis, Stanislaus Zbyszko and Joe Stecher was the most recognized championship. However, the competing titles sowed confusion and prevented nationwide standards from being adopted. In the summer of 1927, newspapers were filled with stories of corruption and match-fixing. For example, an investigating committee of the Illinois legislature uncovered that William Demetral was forced by Chicago promoter Ed White and his partner, Billy Sandow of Kansas City, to put up $5,000 and a quitclaim to his house as a guarantee that he would not defeat Strangler Lewis in a match. In addition, the Louisiana Boxing Commission charged that a match between Londos and Count Zarynoff was rigged because the Golden Greek threw the Cossack too early in the bout. As we have seen, Joe Stecher was recognized by many as the heavyweight champion who successfully defended his title in Memphis when he defeated Dick Daviscourt in May 1927. Despite this solid victory, the Strangler also claimed the heavyweight title. To bolster his claim, Lewis came to Memphis, where he defeated in two easy falls the "Mastodonic young Indian" Jim Clinkstock on November 3, 1927.

Because both grapplers had successfully defended their titles in Memphis, a championship bout was held in St. Louis on February 21, 1927, between Lewis and Stecher. Memphis's Herbert Caldwell traveled to the Gateway City to report on the bout, which was won by the Strangler after securing two out of three falls. The fact that the *Commercial Appeal* sent Caldwell to St. Louis suggests just how important wrestling had become in Memphis during the 1920s. In addition, the bout also solidified Memphis's importance to the national wrestling industry because both grapplers defeated powerful opponents in the Bluff City before the championship match. Although Memphis was an important wrestling town, it did not automatically follow the dictates of the other major promoters. Rentrop signed Strangler Lewis for a match against a Canadian wrestler named Stanley Stasiak in late March 1928. Stasiak attacked Lewis with a wristlock, but the Strangler replied with a punch to the Canadian's chin that allowed him to pin Stasiak to the mat with a reverse body hold and front head lock. The Canadian lay unconscious on the mat for five minutes before he could be revived and carried to the locker room. Meanwhile, Jim Londos struggled on his circuitous route to a championship bout. In March, he barely defeated Pete Sauer, and the following month, he only secured a draw in his match with fellow heavyweight contender John "Nebraska Tigerman" Pesek. The Golden Greek's lackluster performances and the charge that he had thrown a match in Louisiana tarnished his reputation in Memphis, where many fans turned against him. On May 17, 1928, Londos grappled with the Italian Renata Gardini, who was cheered, while boos and jeers were aimed at the Golden Greek. Being mocked did something to Londos—in the first fall, he allowed Gardini to push him into a corner and then kicked him so hard Gardini fell flat on his back. Landing on top of him, Londos used head scissors and bar arm to pin Gardini to the mat. The Italian won the second fall, but Londos came roaring back, employing a flying mare attack and wristlock to win the third fall and the match. Because of these victories, Londos was recognized by many sportswriters as the leading contender for the heavyweight championship held by Strangler Lewis. To force Lewis's hand, Londos fought a match in Philadelphia against another contender, the German Dick Shikat. On the night of the bout, promoters announced

The Auditorium was home to Memphis wrestling from 1925 to 1971.

that if Lewis refused to meet the winner within thirty days, the Pennsylvania and New York Athletic Commissions would crown the victor heavyweight champion. When the Golden Greek defeated Shikat, he demanded an immediate title match. The Strangler ignored him, and Londos turned his attention back to the wrestling mat. In August, he won bouts against Milo Steinborn and Pete Sauer, but still Lewis would not wrestle him.

In the early months of 1929, Londos continued his grueling schedule, which began to take its toll. Seven thousand fans packed the Auditorium to watch the Golden Greek take on the Blond Bohemian Rudy Dusek. It was a pro-Dusek crowd, and they jeered Londos as he avoided being pinned to the mat. Dusek outwrestled the Greek for most of the match, but suddenly Londos exploded with a flying headlock attack that forced Dusek to the mat. After he was slammed to the mat for the fourth time, Dusek rose with clenched fists and punched Londos in the stomach several times, which forced the Greek through the ropes and onto the arena floor. The Bohemian lunged to further his attack, but promoter and referee Charlie Rentrop stopped him. When Londos crawled back into the ring clutching his stomach, Rentrop declared him the winner. On March 9, Londos wrestled in St. Louis, where he suffered a fractured rib, and when he returned to Memphis ten days later to fight Rudy Dusek, his rib had yet to heal, and a doctor forced him to abort the match.

The Golden Greek wasn't in much better shape on April 10 when he finally met Dusek at the Auditorium. The grapplers had agreed that if neither man achieved two falls, the referee would decide who won. Fifty-two minutes into the bout, Londos pinned the Bohemian's shoulders with a body straddle, winning the first fall. Dusek battered the Greek with a combination cradle and back split, also known as a Little Rock Split. Writhing in pain on the mat, Londos lunged toward the ropes when the referee counted him out, which gave the second fall to Dusek. They wrestled a few minutes more, but neither man gained advantage over the other, which led the referee to award the decision to Dusek. Londos was able to defeat the Bohemian in mid-April, but the damage to his reputation seemed insurmountable. He was no longer the king of Memphis wrestling, and the heavyweight title seemed farther away than ever. One month later, however, his fortunes changed again. The Golden Greek defeated Dusek in a match held in Philadelphia and then did the same to former heavyweight champion Stanislaus Zbyszko back in Memphis. A July victory over Italian wrestler Signor Pietro Bacini again secured Londos's place as a major contender for the championship. The Pennsylvania Athletic Commission offered a title bout to Londos and Dick Shikat, which took place on August 23 in Philadelphia. Londos was heavily favored for the match, and when the bout began, the Golden Greek attacked Shikat with a series of headlocks that put the German in jeopardy. Then Shikat grabbed the Greek with a crotch hold and smashed him to the mat. Londos arose from the first crotch hold, but when the Philadelphia German employed a second one, the Golden Greek was in great pain and had to be carried from the ring. As Londos was carried away, Shikat was crowned the heavyweight champion of Pennsylvania and New York and consequently was recognized as the national champ. Shikat defended his title in Memphis on October 3 when he defeated Matros Kirilenko at the Auditorium. While Shikat was successfully defending his title, Londos continued to rack up more victories. He defeated Paul Jones and Kirilenko in November, and the next month he easily beat the "Man Mountain of Wyoming" Jack Wingo.

Although Shikat was the closest thing the country had to a national wrestling champion, it was by no means a settled affair. The American Wrestling Association continued to award titles, while others thought the National Boxing Association should regulate the grappling industry. In January 1930, the NBA formed a wrestling committee that adopted rules governing the sport and created a mechanism whereby bantamweight, middleweight, light heavyweight and heavyweight national champions would be selected. The committee selected five wrestlers eligible to seek the heavyweight title—Jim Londos, Dick Shikat, Pete Sauer, John Pesek and Gus Sonnenberg—and an entrance fee of $5,000 was required for selected matches. The newly formed Shelby County Athletic Commission associated itself with the NBA, giving added weight to its proceedings. Elimination matches between the top contenders for the NBA heavyweight championship were scheduled in several locations around the country, including Memphis.

Dick Shikat met Pete Sauer at the Auditorium in one of the most complicated and disorganized bouts ever held in the Bluff City. The two grappled for an hour and forty-three minutes before Sauer employed a flying mare attack that smashed Shikat into a corner. As Shikat was being flung, his feet flew over his head, which caused him to accidentally kick referee Charlie Rentrop in the skull. Laying dazed on the mat, Rentrop did not witness Sauer pinning Shikat to the deck. "He's down," the crowd screamed as the referee remained dead to the world. Then, just as Rentrop recovered, Shikat wriggled out from under Sauer and pinned him to the mat. Unaware of what happened, Rentrop awarded the fall to Shikat. Bedlam exploded as fans pushed toward the ring to protest. In the audience were two members of the Shelby County Athletic Commission, Joe Bearman and John E. McCall, who declared that, owing to Rentrop's unconsciousness, no fall would be awarded to either wrestler. Toots Mondt, Shikat's manager, told reporters that he would take the matter to court if his boy didn't win the match. Four minutes later, Sauer was moving into a flying mare position when Shikat pinned his opponent with a back body drop. This fall gave Shikat the victory, but Sauer refused to concede defeat. The confusion of the match embittered both grapplers, who pulled out of the title exhibition by refusing to pay the $5,000 entrance fee, as did Sonnenberg. This left Londos and Pesek as the only contenders for the heavyweight title. On March 3, 1930, the National Boxing Association's wrestling committee met in Memphis to plan the title match between Londos and Pesek. Joe Bearman was a member of the committee, which selected Columbus, Ohio, as the site for the bout and scheduled it for early April 1930. A purse of $20,000 split evenly between the two opponents was offered, and Charlie Rentrop was selected to serve as referee. Two weeks later, Pesek was in Nebraska training hard for the bout when he fell off a horse and dislocated his shoulder. The match was then canceled, and the wrestling committee's heavyweight championship contest was left in limbo.

When Dick Shikat pulled out of the NBA's championship series, the wrestling committee suspended him and called for all member organizations not to sanction any match in which he was scheduled to appear. Despite this ruling, Shikat wrestled in St. Louis and New Orleans without action from the NBA. Ever since the unsatisfactory January 16 bout between Shikat and Sauer, enormous pressure had been directed toward the Shelby County Athletic Commission to schedule a rematch. Giving in, the commission scheduled a bout between the two for April 3, 1930. When NBA President Stanley Isaacs learned of the match, he sent a scathing telegram to Secretary John E. McCall. "Shikat under suspension by N.B.A. on account of refusal to enter tournament sponsored by us. Under no circumstances permit this match to be sanctioned by your commission. Efforts being made to undermine N.B.A. in their wrestling program." This ultimatum did not sit well with the Shelby County members, who promptly walked out of the National Boxing Association's wrestling committee. In addition, Memphians Louis Moss, who served as fourth vice-president of the NBA, and Joe Bearman resigned from the organization. A sense of excitement filled the Auditorium when Shikat and Sauer met on April 3. However, their elation was short-lived, as the bout ground to a draw with neither grappler securing a fall.

Meanwhile, Londos continued to wrestle in Memphis, where, during the month of May, he grappled with the Lithuanian Karl Pojello in two well-attended matches. The Golden Greek struggled a bit with the Lithuanian, who captured the first fall. Pojello then applied several flying mares when Londos lay on his back and savagely kicked the Lithuanian in the chin. Falling to the mat, Pojello lay there, unconscious. Londos then picked him up, smashed him down and pinned Pojello to the mat. After the intermission, the referee announced that Pojello could not continue, and Londos was declared the victor. In their second meeting, Londos easily defeated Pojello, which made him an even stronger contender for the heavyweight crown. The problem was that with Pesek injured and Shikat suspended, there was no one the NBA's wrestling committee could match with the Golden Greek. As the wrestling committee worked to save its championship series, Shikat, who claimed to be the heavyweight champ in seventeen states, racked up a string of victories. In Baltimore, he crushed Pat O'Shocker. Then he smashed Rudy Dusek and Mike Romano in New York and Richmond, Virginia. At the end of May, the NBA bowed to the will of wrestling fans and scheduled a championship bout between Londos and Shikat for June 6 in Philadelphia.

A steady summer rain fell when Londos and Shikat climbed into the ring at Philadelphia's city park as twenty thousand fans pierced the air with howls and screams. It did not take long for Londos to take control of the bout by throwing the German to the ground with such a brutal headlock that Shikat nearly slipped into unconsciousness. For what seemed an eternity, Londos applied so much pressure that Shikat could barely move a muscle. An hour and twenty-three minutes into the match, the Golden Greek finished the German off with a Japanese toe hold. Achieving his life's goal, Jim Londos smiled as he was declared the heavyweight wrestling champion of the world. It was not just the Golden Greek's victory, however. Memphis played a vital role in his career, and the city's wrestling fans took pride in the first heavyweight champion to come out of Memphis. Recognizing his debt to Memphis, Londos returned to the city on June 26 to again meet Rudy Dusek. It took the new champ only forty-six minutes to dispatch Dusek with a flying tackle that knocked the Bohemian out. One week later, the Greek met the Irishman Pat O'Shocker, one of the newer wrestlers on the Memphis scene, at Russwood Park. Londos used multiple airplane swings and body slams to disorient O'Shocker and then finished the Irishman off with a Japanese toe hold. Shikat also returned to Memphis, where he defeated Hans Steinke and Rudy Dusek.

Meanwhile, the NBA took steps to gain further control over wrestling in the wake of its crowning Londos heavyweight champion. In September, the NBA created a separate National Wrestling Association to oversee the sport and avoid the confusion of a boxing organization in charge of wrestling. Colonel Harry J. Landry of Friar's Point, Mississippi, was chosen president, and its headquarters was in New Orleans. Memphis played no part in forming the new governing body, but the Shelby County Athletic Commission soon joined the organization, ensuring that Memphis would remain an important wrestling city. In addition, at the end of October its heavyweight champion again wrestled in the Bluff City. In the opposite corner stood the mustachioed Ghafoor Khan, who, it was said, defeated his opponents with his mysterious, hypnotic eyes. Khan's vision didn't help him that night, for Londos twice sent him to the mat. By the end of 1930, Memphis was one of the most important wrestling centers in the United States. At the same time, however, the economy was collapsing because of the Great Depression, testing whether the sport, and the nation, could survive.

Chapter 3
"I DON'T CARE HOW ROUGH THEY GET"
1931-1941

As the 1930s began, the mat game, like the rest of the nation, was on the ropes due to the Great Depression. By the end of 1931, attendance at Memphis wrestling bouts had decreased so much that ticket prices were cut in half, which did not end the slump; there were only 104,655 tickets sold for forty matches that year. The situation worsened in 1932, with forty-seven bouts offered that drew only 89,471 paid attendees. Ticket sales remained anemic throughout the decade; in 1939, Charlie Rentrop offered forty-one bouts that brought in 95,839 sold tickets.

For nearly a decade, there was an agreement between boxing and wrestling promoters that fisticuffs would be held on Mondays and grappling on Thursdays. The agreement held until boxing promoter Billy Haack, whom you will remember tried and failed to muscle his way into the wrestling game, announced a boxing match to be held at the Auditorium on Thursday, January 22. When promoter D.F. Eastman learned of this, he announced his own move to Mondays. Fearing that this feud could erupt into a full-scale business war, the Shelby County Athletic Commission called a meeting of both parties to hash out a compromise. Chairman Joe Bearman sat down with Haack and Eastman, who agreed to stage their events in the Auditorium but swap nights, Mondays for wrestling and Thursdays for boxing. Monday would be wrestling night in Memphis for the rest of the twentieth century. The first Monday night match took place on January 26, 1931, where two new wrestlers, George Manish of Austria and the Texan Paul Jones, met each other in the ring. Jones won the first fall with a hook body scissors, but the Austrian bounced back to defeat the Texan, two falls to one.

As Memphians flocked to the new Monday night wrestling, the National Boxing Association, which had no authority over wrestling, announced that it did not recognize Londos as the nation's heavyweight champion. This gave the old warrior Ed "Strangler" Lewis a small wedge to demand a title bout with the Memphis Greek. The Illinois Athletic Commission supported the Strangler in hopes of bringing the match to the state. Londos refused, claiming that Lewis would first have to defeat Pete Sauer, Dick Shikat and Hans Steinke before he would meet the Strangler. Undeterred by the Golden Greek's rejection, Illinois staged a heavyweight title fight between Lewis and Wladek Zbyszko in Chicago on November 2, 1931. The geriatrics grappled for thirty-six grueling minutes before the Strangler secured two falls against Zbyszko. Crowned Illinois heavyweight champion, Lewis and his management hoped that this gave him enough clout to secure a title match against Londos. However, very few recognized the Strangler as a legitimate champion. New York, which also refused to cooperate with the NWA, crowned Lewis heavyweight champ after he smashed Jack Sherry to the Madison Square Garden mat in 1932. That year, the Strangler also racked up victories over Gino Garibaldi, Rudy Dusek, Pete Sauer and George Zaharias. In his popular column "Wise and Otherwise," Caldwell reported on the Lewis-Sauer bout: "It seems that Sauer ruffled the few remaining strands of the Strangler's hair and the referee, deciding that Sauer was becoming too rough with the old man, declaring Lewis the winner. The old Strangler is getting a bit fragile, and the Garden promoters must preserve his bones—to retain a world's champion of the Garden." Strangler Lewis's desperate bid to remain a viable champion in defiance of age was, for some, a nostalgic trip back to previous decades, while for others like Caldwell, it was an embarrassment that returned wrestling to its seamier past.

While the Strangler clung to his career, Londos continued to defend his title in matches across the country. In July 1931, the Greek returned to Memphis to meet one of the city's up-and-coming grapplers, Pat O'Shocker. The two paired off at Russwood Park on a gloomy night that produced a slippery rain. As thunder punched the night sky, Londos began his attack with two airplane swings and body slams and then stunned O'Shocker with front headlocks before the Irishman came back with a full nelson that the Greek broke with a flying mare. O'Shocker then crashed into the ropes while trying a flying tackle. Londos then employed his Japanese toe hold, which led to O'Shocker's defeat. In mid-December, he returned to the Bluff City to defend his title against Sun Jennings, an American Indian and former

NFL football player. Londos pinned Jennings to the mat with three back body drops for the first fall, and the second came after Jennings employed a head butt that the Greek answered with several headlocks, flying mares and head spins. For the next few years, Londos successfully defended his title in Memphis and throughout the country.

Pat O'Shocker and George Zaharias were two of several new wrestlers who became popular in Memphis during the early 1930s. Described by Herbert Caldwell as a "reckless performer using a flying tackle," George Zaharias, an American of Greek descent from Pueblo, Colorado, arrived in 1929 and slowly made his way up the wrestling pole. The turning point in his career happened when he met Rudy Dusek in September 1931. Zaharias was favored to win, and throughout the match the two pummeled each other mercilessly. Zaharias was especially vicious, beating Dusek with his fists and using a stranglehold. When he kicked Dusek in the stomach, Zaharias was disqualified. The Dusek-Zaharias bout constituted a bit of a sea change for Memphis wrestling—brutal holds and vicious attacks became more prevalent and feuds more pronounced. Wrestlers were not the only ones wanting enhanced violence; the audience became more bloodthirsty as well. When Zaharias met former Illinois football star Jim McMillen on January 4, 1932, the audience was so incensed by Zaharias strangling McMillen about the neck that they threw drink bottles and howled with rage. Herbert Caldwell wrote that "those who heaved the bottles were less sportsmanlike than the wrestler who used a strangle on his opponent." But being a poor sport was the point; it made the matches more dramatic and allowed the fans to emotionally participate in the violence, although throwing glass containers was probably not what the promoters and wrestlers had in mind. In fact, the county athletic commission banned the sale and use of soda bottles during wrestling matches. This did not prevent all ugly encounters between the audience and performers. In the summer of 1933, during a bout between Zaharias and Chief Chewacki, a rabid fan used a handkerchief to conceal a pair of brass knuckles. He punched Chewacki in the face, causing a large gash on his face and forcing him to retire from the match. Three years later, fans nearly rioted when Karl Davis was ruled the victor over Zaharias. It is here that we begin to see the outline of the elaborate storylines and dramatic battles between baby-faces and heels that worked the Memphis audiences into a fever pitch in the years after World War II.

A few weeks after their first meeting, McMillen and Zaharias were scheduled for a rematch. Before they met, however, the Shelby County Athletic Commission weighed in on the growing violence. "I don't care how

Rudy Dusek fought against George Zaharias in one of the most brutal matches Memphis had ever seen.

rough they get, as long as they adhere to the prescribed rules, but if Zaharias continues to willfully violate the rules and ignore cautioning by the referee, it will prove costly to him," explained Chairman Joe Bearman. Six thousand fans crowded into the Auditorium on Monday night, February 1, 1932, to see just how violently Zaharias would act. Employing a series of front headlocks and a body straddle on McMillen, Zaharias took the first fall in only twelve minutes. For the second fall, McMillen slammed Zaharias to the mat several times before pinning his shoulders to the canvas. Then things turned ugly. McMillen lunged into Zaharias, who landed under the ropes. The two smashed into each other with such force that they spilled out of the ring and onto the floor. The former football star was the first to reenter the ring, and when the dazed Zaharias climbed onto to the ring's edge, McMillen rushed the Colorado grappler and exchanged several punches with his opponent until referee Charlie Rentrop ruled McMillen the winner. The following month, Zaharias met the Irishman Pat O'Shocker in a match that ended in a spectacular manner. O'Shocker slammed Zaharias to the mat three times, which dazed the Colorado mauler and forced him under the ropes. As Zaharias moved out from under the ropes, O'Shocker pummeled him with his forearms and elbows. O'Shocker then employed several front headlocks, but it was not enough to overcome the Coloradoan.

Zaharias then met Jim Londos on a Monday night in September at the Auditorium. During the first few minutes of the bout, Zaharias elbowed the heavyweight champ in the jaw and threw the dazed Londos out of the ring. Jumping back into the squared circle, the Golden Greek grabbed the Pueblo challenger in a headlock and threw him across the ring. Grabbing Zaharias in a crotch hold, Londos banged him to the mat but was unable to pin him properly. The Colorado grappler caught Londos in a crotch hold but was barely able to slam him to the mat, which led to the Golden Greek retreating to the ropes. When Zaharias used another crotch hold to pull Londos off the ropes, the heavyweight champ turned the tables on him by falling backward and pinning Zaharias for the first fall. It then took the champ only eleven minutes to win the second fall and the match by propelling the Pueblo mauler out of the ring and into oblivion.

Pat O'Shocker arrived in 1931. In his first match, he was paired against the "Colorado Giant" Floyd Marshall. In his inaugural bout, the red-headed Irishman used a crotch airplane whirl and body slam to wang Floyd Marshall to the mat. In later matches, he was defeated by Pete Sauer and wrestled George Tragos to a draw. O'Shocker was nearly as brutal as Zaharias, and in October 1932, his rough tactics nearly ended his career in Memphis. On

October 3, he wrestled Joe Savoldi, former Notre Dame football player. Twice the Irishman used a clinched fist on Savoldi, for which he was warned by referee Charlie Rentrop. Stunned, Savoldi rolled under the ring and onto the mat ledge when O'Shocker "climbed through the ropes and began bouncing on the former football player as if he was a trampoline," reported Caldwell. Then he repeatedly kicked Savoldi in the head before rolling back into the ring. Because of the Irishman's many fouls, Savoldi was awarded the match. After receiving a report from Deputy Bill Hanna, the Shelby County Athletic Commission suspended O'Shocker for thirty days and levied a twenty-five-dollar fine. The commission declared, "Last night's match clearly showed that the time has come to curb wrestlers…whose very actions are really to incite a mob or a riot. Such actions will not be permitted by the commission.…We realize that the public enjoys these rough matches and so does the commission, but as above stated the safety of the public who attend, must also be considered."

His next match in Memphis was a return contest with Zaharias on November 28, 1932. Zaharias seemed a bit wobbly during the first minutes of the bout, but then the Colorado mauler rolled O'Shocker over the mat six times and used a front headlock to win the first fall. The Irishman secured the second fall when he grabbed Zaharias in a crotch hold and slammed him to the pad three times before pinning his shoulders. For the third fall, the Colorado wrestler made two flying tackles, but on the third try O'Shocker leaped in the air, which broke Zaharias's momentum and led to his head smashing into the Irishman's groin. Falling to the mat, O'Shocker was knocked out, and Zaharias was declared the winner. In March 1933, he met Savoldi again in another violent match. Savoldi secured the victory, but not before O'Shocker smashed the former football star's jaw.

As O'Shocker and Zaharias were building their careers in Memphis, Ed "Strangler" Lewis continued to defend his New York title and hoped for a chance to defeat Londos to become the undisputed heavyweight champion. Age remained the Strangler's biggest problem, as he wrestled younger, and rougher, opponents. Despite this, Lewis remained a wily grappler who often had the sympathy of referees and promoters. A case in point is when he met Pete Sauer, wrestling under the name Ray Steele, at Madison Square Garden at the end of 1932. Neither wrestler distinguished himself in the first half-hour of the match—no falls, leaps or slams, just lackluster performances. No doubt this suited the aging Lewis, but it was frustrating to Sauer/Steele, who reacted by repeatedly hitting the Strangler as they clinched. Seeing these fouls, the referee halted the bout and declared Lewis the winner. As he did this, a Lewis supporter bounded into the ring to protect him, as another fan lunged for promoter Jack Curley. Five police officers protected the promoter while fistfights erupted throughout the Garden. The Strangler continued to rack up victories throughout 1933. In January, he defeated Missouri's Jim Browning at Madison Square Garden and then crushed George Manish at the Memphis Auditorium in October. Flush with victory, Lewis taunted Londos for refusing to meet him.

Meanwhile, the Golden Greek held tight to his world title. In Chicago, he smashed the former champ Joe Stecher with body slams and a reverse headlock. A few weeks later, he returned to Memphis, where he met the challenge of a young wrestler named Whitey Hewitt. Explaining the evolution of professional wrestling into a violent morality play, Caldwell wrote, "Here's a wrestling story in which Jimmy Londos is the hero and Whitey Hewitt is the villain and like all true wrestling stories the villain gets whipped by the hero. In this story the villain gets whipped in the first act but the hero drags him back for another act and whips him all over, much to the satisfaction of the spectators, and there was a happy ending." In April, Londos visited Chicago to grapple with former Notre Dame football player Joe Savoldi. Twenty-six minutes into the match, Londos grabbed Savoldi's arm in a scissors hold. The Notre Dame grappler rose from the mat with the Golden Greek still clinging to his arm. Fighting near the ropes, Savoldi grabbed Londos's legs and stood him on his head. From that position, he rolled the Greek's shoulders on the mat. Referee Bob Manogoff saw Londos's position and quickly declared Savoldi the winner without a count. Even those who hated Londos felt that Manogoff's action was suspect. This feeling only grew when Manogoff announced that Joe Savoldi was the new heavyweight champion. Responding to press and fan attacks, the referee explained that "Londos' shoulders were pinned to the mat. He was down and I called it as I saw it. As far as I am concerned, Savoldi threw him, and he is the champion. I made my decision without fear of partisan reprisals, so-called 'combination' interference or personal gain." However, few believed him.

Some felt that this was a put-up job to remove Londos's crown, while others suggested that Manogoff was paid off or that Londos threw the match to improve attendance at his matches. The Golden Greek insisted that he was not thrown, and the National Wrestling Association adamantly declared that Savoldi was not the heavyweight champion. An investigation was launched by the NWA that found that Londos was not pinned, and even if he was, the match was not a championship bout. During the investigation,

Savoldi insisted that he was champ and refused to wrestle Pat O'Shocker in Evansville, which led to his indefinite suspension from the NWA's Indiana State Athletic Commission.

The NWA's decision quieted the controversy and secured Londos's championship belt. Nine months later, Londos returned to Memphis, where he easily defeated Dr. Karl Sarpolis. On the last day of January 1934, the Golden Greek had a chance to even the score with his rival Joe Savoldi. As twenty thousand fans packed the Chicago stadium, Savoldi busted Londos with a flying tackle and headlock that seemed to stun the Greek. He recovered quickly, though, slamming Savoldi to the mat with a gleeful abandon and finishing him off with a reverse body hold. Any question of who deserved to be called the champ was dispelled that night. Although he frequently wrestled in venues across the nation, Memphis remained important to Jim Londos. In June, four thousand Memphians watched as the Golden Greek went up against former Olympic wrestler Charlie Strack. Back body drops and a straddle disoriented Strack, allowing Londos to win the first fall. After a ten-minute recess, the bell rang, and Strack wobbled out of his corner. Thirty seconds later, he was on his back, being pinned by the Golden Greek. He barely knew what hit him. One month later, Londos did much the same to Ernie Dusek, who was tossed from the ring and pinned with a body slam during a match in Harrisburg, Pennsylvania.

Meanwhile, Strangler Lewis wasn't getting any younger. In December 1933, he grappled in St. Louis with Pete Sauer. The Strangler hoped to crush Sauer as he had George Manish, but this time his luck eluded him when Sauer knocked him out with a right to his chin. Lewis wrestled anywhere that would let him. He even fought in a Mexico City bull ring, where Jim Browning smashed him in two falls out of three. After this defeat, few believed that Londos would ever put up his title in a match against the Strangler. But that is just what he did when he met Lewis at Wrigley Field in Chicago on September 20, 1934. Fifty Memphians, including Charlie Rentrop, took the train to see the bout. At first, the Strangler withstood Londos's assaults with ease, as he placed the Golden Greek in several headlocks that were broken by the champ. As he was placing Londos in another headlock, the Greek turned the tables with a crotch hold and threw Lewis into the ropes. Londos then whipped a hammerlock and three-quarter nelson on the Strangler, who collapsed in defeat. The match was an important moment in professional wrestling history because 35,265 people watched the Londos/Lewis match, 5,000 more than attended the Frank Gotch/George Hackenschmidt championship in 1908.

One Memphian who didn't go to Chicago was sportswriter Herbert Caldwell. No one in Memphis had done more to promote wrestling and make it a true success than Caldwell. In the beginning, he was very critical of the mat game, but over time he became one of its greatest champions. He not only faithfully covered each bout for the *Commercial Appeal*, but Caldwell also reported on the inside maneuverings of promoters and wrestlers. In mid-1935, he retired, and the wrestling beat was given to Early Maxwell. Maxwell didn't really believe that wrestling was a sport, but he dutifully, if without enthusiasm, reported on the mat game. The fact was wrestling no longer needed a newspaper champion like Herbert Caldwell. Love of the mat game was deeply felt in Memphis, and it became even more popular when radio station WHBQ began broadcasting live the Monday night matches at the Auditorium in April 1935.

Despite Maxwell's skepticism, professionals continued to see Memphis as one of the country's important wrestling towns. This was especially true of Jim Londos, who never stayed gone from the Bluff City for very long. One of the most significant matches that took place in Memphis during the 1930s was the bout between the Golden Greek and Jim McMillen during the Memphis Cotton Carnival. Overseeing the affair was carnival king Neely Mallory; his queen, Mollie Darnell; and their royal court. A preliminary match between the "Wild Indian" Chief Chewacki and Bob "Preacher" Savage began the proceedings. Chewacki, who was George Mitchell of Oklahoma, easily dispatched the Preacher with a series of body slams. His victory secured, Chewacki stunned the audience when he walked out of the ring with a bouquet of flowers, which he presented to the Cotton Carnival Queen.

Then Londos and McMillen walked through the boisterous crowd and into the ring. The Golden Greek moved slowly as the bout began and remained on the defensive for much of the match. McMillen smashed into Londos with several flying tackles that the Greek countered with body scissors. Ninety minutes later, the match remained a stalemate, so the referee ruled the bout a draw. Although he didn't lose, the fact that Londos was unable to achieve a clean win suggested that the Greek was beginning to slip. In addition to Cotton Carnival royalty, Damon Runyon, famed sportswriter and author of *Guys and Dolls*, also attended the bout. In his syndicated column, he wrote, "They had a wrestling match…showing that the Memphil have a true appreciation of sport. Your old friend Jeems Londos and Jim McMillen were on the bill. The show was promoted by Charles Rentrop, who has been booking wrestlers in various southern cities a long time."

WRESTLING—WORLD'S CHAMPIONSHIP
FOUR ALL-STAR MATCHES
COTTON CARNIVAL SPORTS FEATURE

JIM LONDOS
CHAMPION
vs.
JIM McMILLEN
CHALLENGER

CHIEF CHEWACKI
WILD INDIAN
vs.
BOB SAVAGE
BEARDED PREACHER

JIM LONDOS

JIM McMILLEN

ELLIS AUDITORIUM — TUESDAY, MAY 7
ADMISSION: $1.65, $1.10, 85c, 55c (Tax included)
ADVANCE SALE—PANTAZE DRUG STORE (Main and Monroe)

One of the greatest wrestling matches of the 1930s occurred between Jim Londos and Jim McMillen during the Memphis Cotton Carnival.

No one knew it, but Londos's time as heavyweight champion was nearly over. Seven weeks after he fought McMillen to a draw in Memphis, he met in Boston a former Irish Free State soldier named Danno O'Mahoney. The Greek's strategy of wearing his opponent down and striking when he was exhausted didn't work on the Irish soldier. O'Mahoney used his Irish whip hold to great effect, knocking Londos off balance. Unable to extricate himself from the soldier's grip, Londos remained pinned to the mat until O'Mahoney was declared the winner. This defeat effectively ended the Golden Greek's career. He never again visited Memphis, although he did occasionally wrestle in between taking care of his avocado ranch in California. It is no exaggeration to state that Jim Londos is the man most responsible for making the mat game a legitimate sport in America. When he started his career in 1914, wrestling was perceived to be crooked and populated with grubby vagabonds who provided cheap spectacle. By the time he lost his title in 1935, wrestling had become accepted as a legitimate athletic contest and was extremely popular throughout the United States.

Charlie Rentrop wasted little time in contacting the new heavyweight champion. An agreement was reached for O'Mahoney to meet Joe Cox of Kansas City on Monday, August 19. The contest was nothing like a

Londos match, but 4,500 Memphians watched as the heavyweight champ used a flying scissors and an airplane swing to defeat Cox in two falls. O'Mahoney returned to Memphis in 1936, defeating Gus Sonnenberg on Monday, February 10. He might not have been as flashy as Londos, but the Irish soldier was a solid draw at the box office—6,000 mat fans watched him smash Sonnenberg. O'Mahoney was unlike Londos in another way; Memphis had little to do with his becoming heavyweight champion and was only one of several stops on the wrestling circuit. Less than a month after his victory over Sonnenberg, O'Mahoney put his title on the line in a bout with former champion Dick Shikat in New York. The elder wrestler slammed into the Irish soldier, employed a hammerlock and pinned O'Mahoney to the mat in a mere eighteen minutes. Meanwhile, back in Memphis, a new grappler who saw himself as a scientific wrestler rather than a showman was gaining a following.

Born in Michigan, Lou Thesz grew up in St. Louis with his Hungarian-born father, who had once been an amateur wrestler. Young Lou learned many holds from his dad, and by the time he turned fourteen, he had dropped out of school to devote himself to professional wrestling. He had his first professional bout in the spring of 1934, and he came to Memphis in December 1935, wrestling in a fifteen-minute match. However, his real debut occurred in April 1936 when he substituted for an ailing Pete Sauer in a match with Dorv Roche. Although he lost the bout, Memphians seemed to like Thesz from the start. His athletic, no-nonsense approach stood in stark contrast with the brutality of O'Shocker and Zaharias and the wild antics of grapplers like Chief Chewacki. On April 20, Thesz failed to withstand the reverse flying scissors, a spread eagle and a body slam from Indiana native Karl Kuss. After this defeat, the Hungarian took what he learned while in Memphis to the western United States, where he scored several victories. The experience he gained out west stood Thesz in good stead when he returned to Memphis on March 2, 1937. The Hungarian slammed Tommy O'Toole in two falls with a flying tackle, body slam and an airplane spin. Thesz wrestled in Memphis several times during 1937, honing his skills while defeating such grapplers as Lew Plumber and Dorv Roche and fighting to a draw with Schniki Shikuma and Jack Humberto.

For the rest of 1937, Thesz made the rounds of the wrestling circuit, building his reputation and his skill set. By the end of the year, he was recognized as a heavyweight contender despite his relative youth. This became apparent in December when Thesz secured a title match with heavyweight champion Everette Marshall. As we have seen, it was rather unusual for someone so

Lou Thesz wrestled several times in Memphis during the 1930s at the start of his successful career.

inexperienced to be given a shot at the title. However, since Londos's defeat, several men had been heavyweight champ, including O'Mahoney, who was defeated by Dick Shikat until Ali Baba took the title from him. On June 26, 1936, Marshall defeated Ali Baba, making him the champ when he met Thesz more than a year later. The two men fought hard, but the Hungarian grappler was able to overcome Marshall to become the American Wrestling Association's heavyweight champion. Two months later, he lost the crown to Steve Casey, but he continued to wrestle at a feverish pace in Memphis and across the nation. Everyone wanted to wrestle the former champ, including several in Memphis. The Hungarian racked up five draws and six wins in 1938, and the following year, he secured four victories in the Bluff City. In February 1939, he again defeated Everette Marshall in St. Louis. This time he kept the title for seven months before being defeated by Bronko Nagurski.

Memphians were very familiar with Nagurski. In the early 1930s, he played football with the Chicago Bears, who made several appearances in the Bluff City. When he turned to the mat game, he wrestled in Memphis many times.

The new champ came to Memphis for a title match in September against Dorv Roche. In many ways, it was a strange bout. Carloss Rodigues of Mexico, instead of Charlie Rentrop, officiated, and he didn't seem to know what he was doing. Bronko won the first fall when he employed a toe hold on Roche after the two broke from a deadlocked double leg cradle. The second fall, and the match, was awarded to Nagurski after Roche refused to abandon a "lethal" boomerang hold. "I never saw such a raw deal in all my life," muttered a female fan as she exited the event. A week later, Rentrop was able to secure a rematch between the two, provided he agreed to act as referee. About 3,500 fans, which was the average attendance for Memphis wrestling matches in the late 1930s, watched Bronko and Dorv struggle to prove who was the better grappler. Blocks were flying around the ring by both men when Roche slammed into Nagurski, who used a flying block to smash Dorv to the mat, where he was easily pinned by the former Chicago Bear. Bronko then stayed close to the ropes as Roche tried to crush him with his boomerang hold. Nagurski quickly turned the tables when he pivoted into an inside toe hold that pulverized Dorv and gave Bronko the second fall and the match. Nagurski hung on to the title until March 1940, when he accepted a title match with Pete Sauer. The two met in St. Louis, where Sauer busted Bronko up and was named heavyweight champion of the NWA. Sauer had wrestled in Memphis for more than a decade, which meant he was the second champion that the Bluff City had helped establish. Five weeks later, the new champ wrestled in Memphis against Dorv Roche, defeating the former Pennsylvania coal miner with an upside-down reverse crab hold. That same night, Lou Thesz, whose stardom had dimmed when he lost the title, grappled with Bill Lee to a draw in the preliminary bout.

Bronko Nagurski captured the NWA heavyweight title during a match in Memphis.

Meanwhile, a new type of wrestling was introduced to Memphis in 1939. Charlie Rentrop scheduled a team match where two grapplers joined forces to oppose another two-man team. The first teams to wrestle in Memphis were Dorv Roche and Dan O'Conner against Charlie Strack and Tom Hanley. To build public excitement, Rentrop hired the former world heavyweight boxing champion Jack Dempsey to referee the bout. On the night of March 20, four thousand fans poured into Ellis Auditorium to see the Manassa Mauler ride herd over the city's first team match. Roche dominated the bout by throwing Strack out of the ring and then head-butted Hanley into submission as O'Conner held him from behind. As he passed through the ropes to reenter the ring, Strack was grabbed by Roche and pinned to the mat. When the first fall was given to Roche and O'Conner, Strack objected to Dempsey's decision. When Strack wouldn't let it go, the former boxing champ landed a fist on the wrestler's jaw, ending his objection. O'Conner took the lead in the second bout, forcing Hanley into the ropes, where O'Conner hung him upside down by his feet before crushing him to the floor. At the same time, Roche used a double-handed back toss to end his opponent and the match.

As we have seen, scientific wrestlers like Lou Thesz despised the outlandish showmanship of grapplers like Ali Baba and Chief Chewacki. In 1940, a new performer arrived on the scene who made these showmen look like rank amateurs. Born in Rheims, France, Maurice Tillet suffered from pituitary overdevelopment that resulted in a larger than normal face and jaws and a massive collarbone and ribcage. He was studied by a team of Harvard University anthropologists, who marveled at his physical development and declared that he was "intelligent, very appealing, kindly and gentle." Tillet's condition was a detriment to the pursuit of many careers, but it was an asset in professional wrestling. Calling himself "The Angel," Tillet electrified the mat game across the nation and piqued the curiosity of Memphis fans who, according to the *Commercial Appeal*, "have been awaiting a chance to get a glimpse of the 'Gable of the groaners,' whose ears are the size of flapjacks and whose nose wired for TVA electricity would make a good sized traffic light." They got their wish when Tillet agreed to meet Gus Sonnenberg on July 22. Many in the crowd of 5,973 gasped as they watched the Angel lumber into the ring. Usually, fans screamed and gestured wildly as they watched the action, but not on this night. The audience sat quietly with only an occasional groan rising from the seats as they watched the Angel crush Sonnenberg with a bear hug. He did it again in October when he brutally squeezed the chest of Ray Villmer in front of 2,000. Attending the Villmer match was the dean of Memphis sportswriters, Walter Stewart, who rarely deigned to cover the mat game but was fascinated by Maurice Tillet. Devoting his daily column to the Angel, Stewart wrote, "So, the Angel came down the aisle with gnarled shoulders aswing—great pincusion [*sic*] hands dangling limp. He came into the ring and attacked a fellow called

Left: Maurice "the Angel" Tillet suffered from pituitary overdevelopment and electrified professional wrestling in the 1940s.

Right: In the 1930s and 1940s, Mildred Burke was the female wrestling champion of the United States.

Ray Villmer. We have long regarded Ray as a brute of the first order, but he seemed an over-civilized child as he skipped about the square and attempted combat. It was a trifle like attacking the side of a concrete pill box with a feather duster."

Maurice Tillet was not the only unusual wrestler to visit Memphis in the early 1940s. For several years, women had been wrestling each other and drawing large crowds. Most fans embraced the idea of women grapplers, but there were those who felt it was downright sinful. Reverend W.E.R. Morrow denounced the practice: "To my mind, nothing is more calculated to degrade human nature to its most bestial depths than the sight of an apparently healthy pair of young women, wearing nothing more than a bathing suit, indulging in the repugnant postures of 'all-in' wrestling." In the 1930s, the most popular female grappler was Mildred Burke, who was crowned female wrestling champion of the United States when she defeated Clara Mortenson in Chattanooga on January 28, 1937. The following year, she participated in a mud wrestling match with Wilma Gordon that was covered by *Life* magazine. It was clear to Charlie Rentrop that Memphians had no qualms about watching women indulge in "repugnant postures," so he secured an appearance by Burke for the weekly Monday night matches at Ellis Auditorium. At her March 10, 1941 Memphis debut, the "Queen of the Ring" defeated her opponent, Gladys Gillem, with a straddle and an alligator hold, which was her own modification of the double jackknife. Burke returned to Memphis several times during 1941, setting the stage for more female wrestling in the future.

On Monday, December 2, the former Pennsylvania miner Dorv Roche met and defeated the masked Irishman who was known only as the Green Shadow. Roche lost the first fall when the Green Shadow employed a body spread but bounced back with a tackle and spread and a back body drop to gain the victory. Five days later, Japan attacked American and British interests in the Pacific, including the naval base at Pearl Harbor. Anxious Memphians listened intently to their radios for news of the battles throughout that Sunday afternoon, and the following day they heard President Franklin Roosevelt ask Congress for a declaration of war against Japan, which was promptly approved. As Memphians anxiously waited to hear from their loved ones and neighbors trapped in the Pacific war zone, several thousand made their way to the Monday night wrestling matches. On December 8, Rudy Strongberg wrestled Bobby Roberts, who was able to win the first fall with a tackle and spread. Strongberg fought back hard, winning the second and third falls and the match. In other bouts, the Green Shadow crushed Soldier Thomas, while Count Von Zuppi of Hamburg, Germany, wrestled Lon Chaney of Hammond, Indiana, to a draw. Two days later, another German, Adolf Hitler, declared war on the United States, calling into question the future of wrestling at a time when real fighting was needed to preserve democracy and the United States.

Chapter 4

"BEAUTIFUL DANCERS, A TALENTED SINGER AND EIGHT BURLY WRESTLERS"

1942–1957

As the war effort increased during 1942, professional wrestling faltered. For example, Rentrop signed a new grappler named Albert Alexinis of Buffalo, New York, but just before the match, he was called before his local draft board and could not appear. In his place, Rentrop found Roy Welch of Oklahoma, who defeated Buddy Knox of Wheeling, West Virginia. At the same time, wrestling lost some of its excitement as many of its fans left for the armed forces and others were working long shifts in war production plants. Even the menace of the alleged German Count Von Zuppi drew only small crowds. However, the situation improved when a new masked grappler called the Golden Terror arrived in the Bluff City. Facing Dorv Roche in his inaugural bout, the Terror used an inside toe hold and three slams and a straddle to dispatch the former miner in a mere sixteen minutes. After achieving fifteen victories in Memphis, the Terror faced former heavyweight champion Ed "Strangler" Lewis. "It was expected that the aging Strangler would easily succumb to the younger Terror, but the fighting heart of the old grappler still beat strong as he entered the ring with his 305-pound opponent. He won the first fall with a series of body slams and a straddle, then the 'Strangler' proved that little of his strength had passed with the years when he clamped on a headlock to take the second fall after four minutes with his famous headlock and then scored the victory with another headlock after nine minutes," reported the *Commercial Appeal*. The

Strangler's victory over the Golden Terror was noticed by everyone in the mat world and gave him another shot at the heavyweight title.

In February 1942, Wild Bill Longson crushed Sandor Szabo for the NWA world heavyweight championship. As we have seen, the heavyweight title holder always made at least one appearance in Memphis, and Longson was no exception. Charlie Rentrop organized a special grappling event to benefit the Army and Navy Relief Funds in August, and to collect as much money as possible, he convinced the new champion to participate. Longson and his opponent, Ronnie Etchinson, gave fans their money's worth with a combination of dramatics and rough stuff. When the bell rang, Wild Bill laid into Etchinson, but when Ronnie returned the favor with a few harsh moves of his own, the champ bolted from the ring, muttering that he "didn't play that way." When Longson returned to the mat, he used a piledriver that secured the match and his victory over Ronnie Etchinson. It was a conquest not only for Wild Bill but also for the Army and Navy Relief Funds, which received $405 for its vital war work. A few months later, Longson lost the title to Bobby Manogoff, whose father had once wrestled Frank Gotch. In December 1942, Rentrop brought Manogoff to Memphis to wrestle Ed Lewis, who had just defeated the Golden Terror a few weeks before. The twenty-four-year-old Manogoff was too much for the aging Strangler. Twenty minutes into the match, Manogoff wrenched Lewis to the mat with an inside toe hold to win the first fall. The younger man's attack was so powerful that the Strangler was forced to throw in the towel and vacate the ring. This was more than a professional victory for Manogoff. Twenty-five years before, the Strangler had crushed the senior Manogoff so brutally that he was forced to retire from the mat game. The fact that these important title matches were held in Memphis again underscores the importance of Memphis to America's professional wrestling industry.

The excitement generated by the Golden Terror and the Strangler improved attendance, as did the introduction of the battle royal to Memphis wrestling. A battle royal consisted of five grapplers in a ring who threw down on each other until the first grappler pinned to the mat is eliminated. The remaining wrestlers continued to tangle until two more had been removed. The last two struggled until one secured a fall against the other. One of the most significant of these events occurred in September 1944 when the Red Angel, Duke Kapalani, Irish Jack Kelley, Jack Wentworth and Babe Zaharias met at the Auditorium. The audience was whipped into a frenzy as they watched the Red Angel, Zaharias and Wentworth tossed from the ring, and Kapalani defeated Kelley with a Hawaiian Stretch. During the

Mae Weston wrestled in Memphis many times during the 1940s.

featured bout between Cowboy Luttrell and Al Massey, the crowd went wild over several decisions made by the referee, Flash Johnson, and rushed the ring. Johnson was injured in the riot, and police were dispatched to restore order. Babe Zaharias agreed to take Johnson's place, and he awarded the match to the Cowboy because Massey wouldn't stop interfering with the ref.

In addition to gimmicks like tag teams and free-for-all matches, Rentrop also began scheduling women wrestlers in his weekly offerings.

In the first female match of World War II, Mae Young and Mae Weston teamed up against Rose Evans and "Hillbilly" Elvira Snodgrass on March 3, 1942. The women were so popular that they became the main event in most of the bouts during the war years. For example, in the fall of 1943, Mildred Burke appeared with Mae Weston in a two-out-of-three, ninety-minute match. It took the ring queen a total of nineteen minutes to bust up Weston with a series of face lifts, a straddle and a variation of an alligator crush the queen called a V-hold. Two months later, Elvira Snodgrass and Weston headlined the Monday night matches at the Auditorium. The Hillbilly defeated Weston in three falls, while in the semifinal bout Mae Young crushed Gladys Gilliam with two straight falls.

Women, for the most part, were treated as real athletes, but they did have to endure the casual sexism of the day, such as this from the *Commercial Appeal*: "The rouge, lipstick, and powder puff will be missing tomorrow night, when the women wrestlers follow the example set by men and try their hands at a tag team match." That bout featured Mae Young and Mae Weston versus Elvira Snodgrass and Birmingham's Gladys Gilliam. Fifteen minutes into the match, Weston smashed Gilliam to the mat with a body slam and straddle. The Birmingham grappler came back with a flying scissors hold to secure the second fall from Weston. In the third round, Snodgrass smashed Young with a series of flying mares that gave the victory to Gilliam and Snodgrass. The women, however, continued to clobber each other long after the bell rang. The melee spilled outside of the ring and into the stands, where fans joined in.

Female grappling was so lucrative that Charlie Rentrop was always looking for new gimmicks to draw the fans. The battle royal held in May with male grapplers had been a success, so Rentrop decided to have one for the women. In September 1944, a battle royal was held with Ann Laverne, Ann Miller, Elvira Snodgrass, Nell Stewart and Mae Young. Miller, Laverne and Stewart were crushed early, leaving Snodgrass and Young to slug it out for the win. Twelve minutes into the match, Young employed a kangaroo kick and straddle to beat the Hillbilly Snodgrass. All these women were well respected, but the most popular woman wrestler remained Mildred Burke, who visited Memphis many times during World War II. On January 30, 1944, she tussled with Snodgrass, who fell to the queen after enduring a body straddle, airplane spin and a jackknife. Six months later, the queen fought the Purple Flash at the auditorium. This time, she relied on several face lifts, a body straddle and her signature alligator clutch to smash the purple-masked grappler into submission. At the end of the year, Burke kept her heavyweight title by securing a straight fall victory over Mae Weston. The queen continued her winning streak in Memphis when she met Mae Young in January 1945. Young successfully used an airplane spin and body slam to pin the champ to the mat, but Burke quickly roared back, thumping Young to the canvas for the second fall. Five minutes later, the queen employed a jackknife for the third fall and victory. Eleven days after World War II ended, female wrestling continued, with June Byers stomping Nell Stewart and Mae Young doing the same for Elvira Snodgrass.

In 1944, Mae Young defeated Elvira Snodgrass in a five-woman battle royal.

While women grapplers climbed to the mat game's top spot, Wild Bill Longson was working to regain the heavyweight belt from Bobby Manogoff. In February 1943, a title match for the two rivals was organized in St. Louis. In a nod to Memphis, Charlie Rentrop was hired to referee the important bout. The two were evenly matched in the first minutes, but according to wrestling historian Ken Zimmerman Jr., "Manogoff exploded with an offense of forearms and his patented kangaroo kick at about the 20-minute mark. Unfortunately, Rentrop was next to Longson and caught the brunt of the move also." As the Memphian sat stunned against the ropes and Manogoff worked to revive him, Wild Bill punched Manogoff upside the head, which caused him to collapse at Rentrop's feet. Not knowing what happened, the Memphian counted Manogoff out and declared Longson the new champion. Fans erupted in anger and rushed toward the ring. The deposed champ's father, Bob Manogoff, kicked Rentrop out of the ring and into the safe arms of several attendants, who carried him away from the mob. The new heavyweight champ returned to Memphis in March, where he successfully defended his title against Dorv Roche. From the spring of 1943 to August 1945, Wild Bill Longson performed in Memphis thirteen times, winning every bout to retain his heavyweight belt.

As Longson was racking up his victories in the Bluff City, Charlie Rentrop was approached by the War Department to teach hand-to-hand combat to soldiers at Lambert Field in St. Louis. In an interview with sportswriter David Bloom, he stated, "I'm going to give a course in commando. They've wanted me up there for some time." Rentrop then explained, "I go out to watch some of these instructors at the camps and the commanding officer asks me what I think of it. Well, I think maybe if some of these boys try that stuff when it counts, they'll get hurt. But I don't say much, just tell them that I'll show 'em my method." In 1944, Rentrop had to use a different kind of method to fight off the advances of Nashville promoter Nick Gulas. For decades, the American Legion had sponsored Monday night wrestling, which helped Rentrop secure the best wrestlers for Memphis. When Rentrop's contract ended in the summer of 1944, Gulas announced that he planned to exhibit wrestling in Memphis on either Wednesday or Thursday nights. This was apparently a ploy to convince the American Legion to drop Rentrop and sign a contract with him. When Rentrop met with the Legion's athletic committee chairman, Mark Heffernan, the two quickly sealed a contract that froze Gulas out of Memphis.

Two months after the war ended, Rentrop signed former heavyweight champion Dick Shikat for a return to Memphis. To sweeten the deal, Rentrop promised that whoever won the match, Shikat or his opponent, Vic Christy, would be given a title bout with Longson. Unfortunately for Christy, his skin broke open with boils, and he was forced to withdraw. He was replaced with Abe Yourist from Syracuse, New York, who met Shikat on October 22. The former champ made quick work of Yourist, who suffered two falls from a back body slam and a leg lock. The long-awaited match between Christy and Shikat took place in December to decide who would challenge Wild Bill. In the first fall, Shikat was disqualified for hitting the referee, then Christy came off the ropes and pinned the former champ with leg scissors that gave him the victory and a shot at Longson. One week later, the less experienced Christy tasted defeat when he aimed a kangaroo kick at Wild Bill that failed to connect. As a result of this misstep, Christy fell to the mat and dislocated his shoulder.

At the same time, Mildred Burke continued to successfully defend her heavyweight belt in Memphis during the early postwar years. For example, she shared the main event with Wild Bill Longson when he defeated Ralph Garibaldi on October 14, 1946. It took her twelve minutes to secure two falls against Juanita Coffman with two straddles and a body slam. The queen visited the Bluff City at least once a year during the late 1940s and early

1950s. No one knew it at the time, but her final visit to Memphis occurred on October 5, 1953, where she again shared the card with Wild Bill Longson. Both grapplers easily won their bouts, but when not in the ring, Burke was on the ropes and couldn't escape. Deeply in debt and hounded by enemies within the wrestling business, she tussled for the last time on July 18, 1955, in Reno, Nevada, where she defeated Ruth Boatcallie in three falls. Mildred Burke's retirement came at a point where women wrestling was becoming less popular in Memphis. Female matches still took place in the 1950s, but not many, and they were no longer a main draw. As the Queen of the Ring's career was entering its final phase and Wild Bill clung to the heavyweight title, a new wrestling sensation arrived in Memphis.

Buddy "Nature Boy" Rogers represented the mat game's return to sensationalism. "He really wasn't that good of a hand, but he was a hell of a showman. He could draw houses where other guys couldn't. He just had that thing. He had a way of making those people want to kill him, and he could do it just with a look, a posture," explained wrestler Don Leo Jonathan. Rogers established the persona of a villain, called a heel in wrestling circles, that fans loved to boo, insult and shake their fists at. Other wrestlers had used this image before, but through the strength of his personality the Nature Boy took it to a new level. Female Memphians were especially drawn to him; the *Commercial Appeal* described him as "the heartbeat of women wrestling fans." His villainous behavior was on full display when he was in Memphis. During his match with Frank Marconi, he severely injured the Italian's neck, which forced Marconi to withdraw, and he dislocated the shoulder of former heavyweight champ Danno O'Mahoney. Because of his popularity, he was given the opportunity to challenge heavyweight champion Wild Bill Longson in December 1946. As 4,500 screaming fans watched, twenty-eight minutes into the bout Longson slapped a flying tackle on Rogers that tossed him from the ring and damaged his shoulder. Wild Bill was awarded the match when the Nature Boy couldn't continue.

As Buddy Rogers drove women wild and Wild Bill clung to his belt, Lou Thesz returned to Memphis after spending most of World War II wrestling in Texas and other points north and west. On June 17, 1946, he partnered with Ralph Garibaldi in a tag team match with Big Ben Morgan and the Green Dragon. The match soon turned rough when Morgan hit the referee and choked Thesz. This gave Thesz and Garibaldi the first fall. Then Garibaldi gained the second when he stunned the Green Dragon with a forearm blow and pinned him to the mat with a straddle. Two weeks later, the former champ crushed Big Ben with a kangaroo kick and finished him

"Nature Boy" Buddy Rogers represented the mat game's return to showmanship.

off with a straddle. Thesz's goal was to recapture the National Wrestling Association's heavyweight championship. His two victories in Memphis, combined with key wins against Ernie Dusek, Warren Bockwinkel and Bobby Manogoff, gave Lou the momentum to challenge Wild Bill for the heavyweight belt. Before he could do so, Longson was defeated by the

Canadian champion "Whipper" Bill Watson in February 1947 in St. Louis. A few weeks after Watson's triumph, Thesz returned to Memphis, where he scored two falls against Eddie Meske with a hammerlock and windmill. One month later, he fought in St. Louis, where he crushed the Whipper to regain the association's heavyweight belt.

Lou Thesz hated the Nature Boy. As a believer in scientific wrestling, he deplored Rogers's showmanship and didn't respect his ability. When the Nature Boy insulted Thesz's mentor, Strangler Lewis, a grudge was born that never really died. The two met in Memphis for the first time on September 29, 1947. Rogers quickly used a jacknife to gain the first fall, which Thesz answered with an airplane spin that dazed the Nature Boy and gave the champ the second fall. Neither grappler was able to snatch a third fall, which forced the referee to declare a draw. Thesz not only held on to his title, but he also took the measure of the Nature Boy and filed it away for future use. The heavyweight champion then turned his attention to his former tag team partner Ralph Garibaldi. Thesz made easy work of the St. Louis Italian, using a drop kick to the chin and straddle to capture two falls out of three. At the end of November, Thesz again put his belt on the line in a rematch against Wild Bill in St. Louis. Almost 9,800 fans watched as Wild Bill came

Lou Thesz wrestling Buddy Rogers. Thesz deplored Rogers's showmanship and didn't respect his ability.

from behind to defeat the younger grappler and recapture the heavyweight championship. Longson did not hold on to the belt for very long, as he lost it to Thesz during a title match in Indianapolis.

This back and forth between the two seasoned grapplers created a lot of heat for Memphis wrestling fans, who flocked to Ellis Auditorium several times in 1948 to see who would retain the title. At their first match of the year, 3,800 fans watched the next chapter in the Longson/Thesz feud. They certainly got their money's worth that night. Wild Bill captured the first fall when he used a piledriver to stun Thesz before being pinned to the mat. Thesz quickly recovered to whip Longson into submission with a drop kick and a straddle. As the third fall began, Thesz attempted to lift Wild Bill into the air for a spin when Longson's foot caught on the top rope. This upset Lou's balance, and the two sprawled out of the ring and onto the concrete floor. Both were knocked unconscious, and when neither awoke during a twenty-count, the bout was declared a draw. At their second meeting, each grappler secured one fall, but then Wild Bill employed a piledriver. When the referee objected, Longson threw him and Thesz out of the ring and was disqualified. Their third meeting in December was just as dramatic as the first two. Fourteen minutes into the match, Longson pinned Thesz with a straddle after slamming his body to the mat. Two minutes later, Thesz roared back with a series of drop kicks that smashed Wild Bill to the canvas. Keeping a close watch on the grapplers was Jack Sharkey, former heavyweight boxing champion. When Longson trapped Thesz in a brutal hold and refused to break it, Sharkey hauled off and thumped him in the skull. As he fell, Thesz pinned him to the mat, gaining the third fall and the victory.

Between the first and second Longson/Thesz matches, several events took place that transformed Memphis wrestling for the rest of the century. First, after twenty-two years in the mat game, Charlie Rentrop announced that he had sold his business and was retiring. In early 1948, he had suffered a heart attack, and this led to his decision to leave the world of professional wrestling. Offers had been coming in to buy the business, including one from former champion Dick Shikat. However, he sold his enterprise to two Tulsa, Oklahoma promoters, Sam Abey and Les Wolfe. No one had done more to establish Memphis as a wrestling town than Rentrop. He booked the best wrestlers, guided Jim Londos's time in Memphis and created an atmosphere of drama and excitement that pulled fans into the culture of wrestling. Rentrop and sportswriter Herbert Caldwell were the ones who put Memphis on the professional wrestling map. A few weeks after Rentrop retired, a consortium of promoters formed the National Wrestling Alliance to protect existing wrestling territories, build cooperation, recognize one heavyweight champion and regulate the behavior of wrestlers. In September, the new organization named Orville Brown as its inaugural heavyweight champion.

Lou Thesz was having none of this Alliance nonsense. He was already champion, and his business relationship with promoters in Memphis, St. Louis and other major markets made him think that he could stay out of the organization. However, many of them joined the Alliance, including Memphis's Les Wolfe; in the summer of 1949, Thesz joined the Alliance and agreed to wrestle Brown for the championship. Then the whole relationship was upended when Orville Brown died in a car accident three weeks before the scheduled match. During their first annual convention in St. Louis, the assembled members named Thesz's old mentor and former heavyweight champion Strangler Lewis to the chairmanship. The Strangler insisted that a new champion had to be selected, and the board unanimously chose Thesz. Meanwhile, the old National Wrestling Association dissolved, leaving the Alliance as the only nationwide wrestling organization and Lou Thesz its undisputed champ.

Television also had a profound effect on the future of Memphis wrestling. Promoter Les Wolfe understood the medium's power, and when it was announced that TV would begin broadcasting in Memphis on December 11, 1948, he moved quickly to secure a spot for professional wrestling. Wolfe hoped that television would excite new fans to attend matches in person. The first wrestling bout broadcast over television in Memphis was the December 20 match between Longson and Thesz where Wild Bill threw both referee and champion out of the ring. In less than a month, these weekly TV broadcasts not only became very popular but also increased attendance. Walter Stewart wrote in his daily sports column, "For some time now, the Commercial Appeal's Station WMCT has focused bland glass eyes upon the weekly wrestling rodeo at the Auditorium. It was freely predicted that the apes of wrath would wither on the vine, but Mr. Les Wolfe, who is chiefly responsible for these uncivilized capers, tells us that the paying multitudes have increased delightfully."

By late August 1949, eighty-two thousand people weekly watched professional wrestling on Memphis television. The relationship between TV and wrestling in Memphis continued for nearly fifty years and benefited both industries. Older wrestlers didn't quite understand this. Even the Nature Boy Buddy Rogers didn't fully understand the power of TV to craft a persona that could be used to not only bring heat while in the ring but also promote upcoming matches. The first wrestler to really understand this was a young man from Texas named George Raymond Wagner. Born in Nebraska and raised in Houston, Wagner began wrestling while still a teenager and quickly became a local favorite. He then moved to California and appeared regularly on Los Angeles television as "Gorgeous George," a wrestler who spent more time having his curly blond hair properly coiffed than he did training for matches. He told one newspaper reporter, "I like the finer things in life. It isn't an affectation; it is natural and normal. Dirt, sweat—ugh!" George quickly rose from local TV to national broadcasts with Bob Hope and appearing in movies. The Gorgeous One took Memphis by storm when he arrived on November 6, 1948, for a bout with Wild Red Berry.

George and his valet, Jeffries, checked into the Peabody Hotel late on a Saturday night. Early the next morning, he took a stroll around the city, with Jeffries following behind spraying a disinfectant to protect the star from being contaminated. Later, he visited the Claridge Beauty Salon, where owner Dorothy Rogers worked on his hair and Annabell Wilson manicured his fingernails. The Gorgeous One's activities were carefully recorded by a *Commercial Appeal* reporter, who wrote that the "Beau Gallant of the grappling game was undecided last night as to his ring attire. He couldn't make up his mind between lavender trunks or the seafoam green pair. He may even wear his newest robe, the solid black one with ermine trimmings. It all depends on what mood he's in." George was in a good mood the next night when he faced Wild Red Berry at the Auditorium. Nine minutes into the bout, the Beau Gallant employed a body twist and straddle to pin Berry for the first fall. Wild Red answered with a body straddle to gain the second fall, although it took him forty-five minutes to pin George to the canvas. Six minutes later, the Gorgeous One repeated his body twist and straddle

Gorgeous George took Memphis by storm when he arrived on November 6, 1948.

to pin Berry for the third fall to secure a victory. Fans were hungry to know more about Gorgeous George, and the press obliged.

Four weeks later, George came back to Memphis to face the Red Shadow. Walter Stewart covered the match for his daily sports column and had the opportunity to briefly meet Gorgeous George. "A pleasure, I assure you," said George as he shook the sportswriter's hand. He then pinned a gold-plated bobby-pin to Stewart's lapel. "Here is a Georgie Pin. Wear it with honor." Jeffries entered the ring first, carrying a tray that included sprayers and face cream. He spread out a towel and a small oriental rug and then began spraying the ring. When satisfied that the ring was decontaminated, he signaled Gorgeous George to enter. Jeffries removed George's hairnet and bobby pins and then gave his coiffure a few strokes with a comb. The bell rang and the match began. The Shadow went straight for George's hair, yanking it hard until the Gorgeous One jerked away. Red Shadow then employed a Japanese toe hold that George was unable to overcome. After losing the fall, George retreated to his corner, where Jeffries applied lotions and gave him vitamins that appeared to revive the Beau Gallant. Charging out of the corner, George, in the colorful words of Walter Stewart, "Rearranged the Red Shadow's brains with two headlocks trimmed with legs flung upward to a point dangerously near the overhead lamps." As a result, the Gorgeous One won the second fall, but he lost the match when his legs became entangled in the ropes. When Gorgeous George came to Memphis, he often pulled a stunt that piqued reporters' interest and ginned up the fans. For example, in July 1950, he was matched against Farmer Jones, who carried a small pig with him before the bout. In full view of a newspaper photographer, a fight nearly broke out between George and Jones when Jeffries moved to disinfect the pig. After the Gorgeous One and his valet went through their usual routine in the ring, Farmer Jones entered with two squealing pigs. Jeffries sauntered over to Jones's corner to disinfect it, but the Farmer refused. Despite the hygiene level not being what George was accustomed to, he still managed to crush Farmer Jones in two falls out of three.

It was science versus showmanship when the Beau Gallant faced heavyweight champion Lou Thesz at the Auditorium on Monday, March 7, 1955. Thesz lunged from the ropes to pin George with a flying body straddle. In the second fall, the Gorgeous One turned the tables on the champ with a rocking leg lock, but Thesz came back quickly with a drop kick and body press to win the third fall and the match. Once he dispatched Gorgeous George, the scientific champ continued to defend his title across the United States. He returned to Memphis in July, squaring off against former champion Bobby Manogoff. The relentless schedule began to slowly wear Lou down; he was only able to achieve a draw against Manogoff, and the following year in St. Louis, he lost the crown to Whipper Billy Watson. The new champion defended his title for the first time during the annual Cotton Carnival in Memphis. In his match against Ike Eakins, the Whipper scored two falls to keep the heavyweight belt. Lou Thesz visited Memphis three months later, where he smashed Frank Hewitt in two quick falls. These two bouts set the stage for Thesz and Watson to meet in St. Louis for a title rematch in early November 1956. It took Thesz thirty-seven minutes, five seconds and a savage kangaroo kick to reclaim the title of heavyweight champion of the world.

By the mid-1950s, professional wrestling in Memphis had become more than a mere sporting event. It was now a part of the city's folk culture. One did not even have to be a fan for it to be a part of your daily life. Memphians came to identify with the sport as they did with the blues music that had defined the city for the past fifty years. The best early example of this evolution came in late December 1955 when Les Wolfe offered wrestling matches and other forms of entertainment to raise funds for local Christmas charities. In between matches, the Dixie Dolls dancing troupe, Slim Rhodes and His Mountaineers and the city's newest musical sensation, Elvis Presley, performed in between bouts that featured Wild Bill Longson, Bobby Manogoff and several other grapplers. The *Commercial Appeal* promoted the event as offering "beautiful dancers, a talented singer and eight burly wrestlers." Music and fighting—you can't get more Memphis than that.

Lou Thesz returned to Memphis on April 8, 1957, to defend his title against George Bollas, who wrestled under the mask of the Zebra Kid. Thesz had no trouble disposing of the Zebra Kid, who returned to the Bluff City at the end of the month to face the Nature Boy Buddy Rogers. The Zebra captured the first fall with a head butt and body press. The Nature Boy replied by throwing the kid out of the ring and joining him in the aisle. The Zebra Kid started running down the aisle, with Rogers close behind. The Nature Boy caught up with him outside the Auditorium in the middle of the intersection of Main and Exchange Streets. Whaling on each other, Rogers gained the upper hand and slammed the Kid to the pavement. Then the Nature Boy chased the Zebra back into the Auditorium, where a fan passed him a metal folding chair. Rogers busted it upside the Zebra Kid's head, and the match came to a raucous end. Police held Rogers in custody until it was determined that the Kid sustained no lasting damage. Both men forfeited their fees and were disqualified. At the same time, a new wrestler was slowly gaining popularity in Memphis.

Born Henry L. Faggart in China Grove, North Carolina, Jackie Fargo wrestled in South Carolina and New York before first wrestling in Memphis in the fall of 1953. Fargo first gained notice in Memphis when he joined with his "brother" Don Fargo (in reality a German immigrant named Don Kalt) to compete in a tag team match against the Nature Boy and Country Boy Calhoun on June 3, 1957. Rogers used a sleeper hold on Fargo to gain the first fall, but he bounced back with a body press, drop kick and knee drop to win the second fall from Calhoun. Then things turned ugly. All four rushed into the ring, smashing each other to a bloody pulp. When referee Lou Plummer finally restored order, the Fargo brothers, the Nature Boy and Calhoun stood there dripping with blood as the ref stopped the melee and declared that no one achieved victory. Memphis fans loved this sort of brutality, and they looked to Jackie Fargo to provide it for them.

Meanwhile, the mat game continued to evolve. Since the creation of the National Wrestling Alliance, the business was dominated by promoters who controlled a large territory rather than one town like Les Wolfe did Memphis. It was getting harder for single promoters to compete with the territories. In Tennessee, Nashville promoter Nick Gulas and Roy Welch controlled most of the state save Memphis. As we have seen, Gulas tried and failed to take over Memphis wrestling from Charlie Rentrop in 1944, but in 1957, he was in a much stronger position to try again. At the same time, Wolfe was growing weary of the game. "I've had it," Wolfe exclaimed. In July, he sold his business to Gulas and Welch, who added Memphis to their territory, giving them more control over Tennessee. This also opened more talent to wrestle in the Bluff City. What consequences this would have been was not entirely clear when the year 1957 ended.

Chapter 5
"THESE BOYS ARE SPUTNIK'S BOYS"
1958–1971

He was "235 pounds of twisted steel and sex appeal with the body women love, and men fear." He had a streak of white in the middle of his dark hair and carried the unlikely name of Sputnik.

On December 18, 1928, Roscoe Monroe Brumbaugh was born in Dodge City, Kansas. He drifted into carnival life after service in the U.S. Navy and soon began wrestling professionally. Brumbaugh did not carry with him the casual racism that infected so many other white Americans. He treated Black people no different and was quite willing to flaunt southern racial mores. In 1957, he was driving from Washington State to Atlanta for a TV appearance when he picked up an African American hitchhiker to help with the drive. "We get to Atlanta, and I direct the kid to the television station. He realizes I'm some sort of star or something and begins opening doors for me and unloading my luggage and gear. Then some old hag made a remark about 'my n***er boy.' I made a remark to her, and she called me a 'goddamned Sputnik.' I was Sputnik Monroe from now on." Sputnik's first match in Memphis took place at the annual Christmas charity event, where he defeated Don Fields in what the *Commercial Appeal* described as a "bloody decision." On December 30, 1958, he tried to capture the southern junior heavyweight championship from Yvonne Roberre but was disqualified when he stomped the referee to the mat. In these first two matches, we see a bit of the 1930s heels Pat O'Shocker and George Zaharias in the way Sputnik handled himself in the ring.

Sputnik Monroe flaunted southern racial mores whenever he saw fit.

Sputnik's arrival in Memphis coincided with a change in how local television broadcast wrestling. Instead of covering the Monday night matches at the Auditorium, station managers at WMCT brought wrestling into the studio for a Saturday afternoon program. It's not clear exactly why this decision was made, but it must have had something to do with time. It was never known just how long the Auditorium bouts would last; in fact, some would continue into the wee morning hours. This way the station could keep wrestling to a one-hour format, which was easier for capturing sponsors and new fans. For the mat game, TV helped advertise the Monday night contests while giving the wrestlers an opportunity to build their image and carry on feuds with other professionals. The first show was broadcast on Saturday, February 7, 1959, at 5:00 p.m., and it quickly became a staple of local television. It exposed many people to wrestling who couldn't, or wouldn't, attend a Monday night match at the Auditorium. Wrestling became so ingrained in Memphis culture that it often was discussed with the same intensity as religion and politics. For example, a viewer wrote into the *Commercial Appeal*'s TV Key Mailbag with this question: "After watching wrestling shows on television for some time, now an argument came up between two other boys and I. One says the wrestlers are fake, and no one really gets hurt. Another boy says the whole thing is on the level. I say some of the wrestlers are fake, while others are really out to hurt the opponent. Who's right?" In reply, the editor stated, "If wrestlers really did what wrestlers seem to do on that TV screen, the ring would be strewn with bodies and each bout would be sponsored by a mortuary." Had they asked wrestler Billy Wicks, he would have set them straight. "What I can't understand is why people think all that blood is a fake. That stuff running down my face…wasn't ketchup."

In front of a large crowd at the Auditorium, Sputnik fought his first important Memphis bout when he faced Wicks on April 6, 1959. Wicks won the first fall, but Sputnik savagely attacked him with several blows to the head, a few body slams and a body straddle to win two falls and the match. This first meeting between Billy Wicks and Sputnik Monroe was far more than a wrestling contest. It spawned a glorious feud that played out at the Auditorium on Monday nights, TV screens on Saturdays and in the living rooms and at the supper tables of many Memphians. Billy Wicks was the All-American hero or baby-face, defending Mom, apple pie and the flag; he stood against the bruiser with a Russian name who played dirty and consorted with Black people.

Television did the most to promote the feud. One Saturday afternoon at WMCT's studio, host Jack Eaton was calling a match between Sputnik and Wicks when things turned ugly. "When Monroe slammed Billy Wicks on the concrete floor, I went crazy. I just lost it, and Monroe was a Communist, the worst person…all this stuff. I thought to myself, 'Hey, this could really be something, that we can keep going, a weekly thing like a soap opera.'" Memphians ate it up. According to Wicks, "[With the] local television promoting Sputnik and Billy Wicks, the crowd started coming to 1,000, 2,000, 3,000 and we started filling that place up." With Jack Eaton egging the grapplers on, the feud reached a new level in the summer of 1959. At the end of June, the two rivals competed for the Tennessee state championship in a bloody affair that ended with Wicks gaining the crown. Then in July, Wicks was in the ring with another heel named Butch Boyette when Sputnik suddenly appeared. Boyette was bleeding from a cut above his eye as Wicks was pounding on him. Suddenly, Sputnik vaulted into the squared circle, pushed Boyette away and thumped Wicks until the referee called the match a draw.

The feud between Billy Wicks and Sputnik Monroe was the first great storyline in Memphis wrestling history.

Three weeks later, more than ten thousand fans watched the rivals slug it out again for the Tennessee heavyweight championship. Sputnik won the first fall with several knee drops and a body press and then Wicks pinned Monroe to the mat with a flying drop kick. During the third fall, Sputnik trapped Wicks in one of the ring's corners when another wrestler, Treacherous Phillips, reached between the ropes and jerked Wicks to the mat. Then Sputnik pinned Wicks to the canvas and won the state belt, but Billy blamed Phillips for his loss and demanded a chance to get even. He got his wish when he faced the Treacherous one and crushed him handily. The heat continued to rise as fans watched, screamed and argued about who deserved the title and just how evil Sputnik really was. The feud reached a fever pitch when a grudge match was scheduled for August 17, 1959, at Russwood Park baseball stadium, where Jack Eaton's soap opera drew 13,749 paying customers. In addition to Wicks and Sputnik, the crowd was also excited to see the referee, boxing great Rocky Marciano. The bell rang, the crowd cheered and the two bitter rivals shellacked each other until a grappler named Chico Cortez bounded into the ring to help Sputnik. Marciano smashed Cortez in the face to get him off Wicks, and when Sputnik objected, the retired champ did the same for him. Marciano then ended the match and declared that no decision could be reached. Both men claimed they held the Tennessee wrestling championship, but Rocky Marciano reported to the NWA that neither grappler was entitled to the belt. So, a rematch was scheduled in September with the title up for grabs. As the bout reached its climax, Wicks took a page from Sputnik's playbook when he smashed Monroe with a series of closed fists and then rapped his knuckles into the face of referee Phil Golden. Sputnik then won the belt when Golden disqualified Wicks.

A few weeks later, Monroe attended the Mid-South Fair at the Memphis Fairgrounds. Sporting a black suit, a black derby hat and his state championship belt, he looked a bit like Gene Barry, star of the NBC-TV program *Bat Masterson*, who was also at the fair that day. Sputnik strolled the grounds drawing attention to himself, pretending to wrestle all comers and hatching schemes to become even more famous. That evening, he made his way to the back of the Indoor Arena where Gene Barry was performing at the rodeo. Sputnik had a vague plan of walking into the building, pulling Barry off his horse and punching him in the nose. That way, he thought, "I'd get a national reputation." But it didn't happen. Given his near-legendary status in Memphis, it is hard to accept that Monroe couldn't have gotten into the arena, and near Barry, if he really wanted to. According to Billy Wicks, Sputnik told him, "I just couldn't get up enough nerve." Instead, he spied two African Americans shining shoes, so he started loudly promoting their business. Nearby were a few cowboys and their wives, who objected to Sputnik's boisterous language and asked him to stop. When he didn't, Ray "Kid" Marley of Paris, Tennessee, punched Monroe in the face, leaving a large gash under his left eye. Taken to St. Joseph's Hospital, Sputnik declared that he could "lick any cowboy that ever lived.…I'm a good-looking boy when I'm healed—and I heal fast. When I finish healing, I'll probably go back to the rodeo and straighten things out." First, he had to defend his state title against the Mighty Yankee. In the first fall, the Yank got the better of Monroe with a body press, but Sputnik returned the favor with body slams and a giant knee drop. The third fall, and the belt, went to the Mighty Yankee when Sputnik was counted out while outside of the ring. At the same time, Gulas and Welch's Memphis promoter, Buddy Fuller, smelled money in the rodeo incident. He asked Marley to meet Monroe in the ring the following Monday night, but the cowboy refused. However, many wrestling fans came out anyway in the hopes he'd change his mind. Kid Marley never showed, but another resident of Paris, Tennessee, Jimmy Jones, challenged Sputnik, and the two briefly wrestled before the grappler defeated the amateur with a body press. One week later, Wicks gained the Tennessee Wrestling Championship when he defeated the Mighty Yankee.

Sputnik's concern for the plight of Black Americans and hatred of segregation was genuine, but like with the Kid Marley incident, challenging white supremacy was also good for business. At 12:30 a.m. on Wednesday, January 13, 1960, Sputnik and a fellow white wrestler named Clinton M. Hickman were sipping beers at the counter of Red Johnny's place on Beale Street when police officers walked in and arrested them. Never willing to do the conventional thing, Sputnik hired African American attorney Russell Sugarmon to represent him at city court that morning. Judge Beverly Boushe presided over the trial, where he remarked that this was the first time a Black lawyer had defended a white person in a Memphis court. Speaking to the charges of disorderly conduct, Sugarmon argued that Sputnik had a right to be in a tavern open to the public. Sugarmon also stated that since Monroe had a large African American fan base, he wanted to mingle with them while also patronizing Black-operated businesses. It spread goodwill and helped build Sputnik's own enterprise. Not surprisingly, Judge Boushe ruled against Sputnik, stating that the disorderly conduct ordinance contained a section that defines the statute as "anything offensive to others." His opinion then noted, "I am sure the incident can be considered offensive to the great majority of Memphians of both races." Sputnik paid the twenty-six-dollar fine but remained defiant: "[This] must be some kind of a Communist inspired deal, and I can't go where I wanna go, I'm a veteran of a war and the toughest son of a bitch you ever saw in your life, and I can't go where I wanna go?" Sputnik later claimed that he went back to Beale Street again, and there is little doubt that he did. However, the police must have left him alone. The owner of Red Johnny's, John Brown, did not fare as well. He was warned by the City Licensing Commission not to sell beer to any other white people. This increased scrutiny led to his liquor license being suspended for four months when Brown was involved in a fight.

In late 1959, studio wrestling moved from WMCT to WHBQ-TV, which added an audience to the show. Sputnik appeared on one program in April 1960, where he said something that was deemed "off-color" by the viewing audience. To make matters worse, most of the audience were grade-school children. The station received many phone calls from irate viewers, which forced Fuller and WHBQ program director Gene Roper to ban Sputnik from the Memphis airwaves. Being pulled from TV did little to hurt his reputation; in fact, it probably helped it. In June, the Delphi Youth Club, an African American club in North Memphis, held a series of events to encourage Black teenagers to, in the words of police lieutenant E.H. Harrison, "set a big goal for yourself, demand the best, but be yourself." There was no one in Memphis who followed the creed of "be yourself" more than Sputnik, which he showed by leading a parade down the streets of North Memphis. Monroe's angry fight against segregation increased as more and more Black Memphians clamored to see him in person. He despised the fact that Black attendance was severely restricted to the cramped balcony, far away from him. Auditorium leaders slightly gave in to Sputnik when a "special Negro Section" was opened for Black citizens in March 1959. With this small victory, Monroe devised a plan to further circumvent segregation and improve the lot of his fans. According to Jim Dickinson, a white teenager who adored Sputnik and later became a world-renowned rock-and-roll music producer, "They had a guy counting the white door and a guy on the back door. And they knew how many blacks the section could hold. Sputnik paid the guy who counted the blacks to say a low number every time he was asked....Finally the audience got so big and so heavily black that they had to integrate the seating." Black Memphians never forgot how Sputnik stood up for them. Johnny Dark, founder and president of the Sputnik Monroe Fan Club and a respected Memphis broadcaster, was traveling with him in Louisville, Kentucky, when, an elderly Black woman approached him with tears rolling down her cheeks. "She said, 'You don't remember me, you never met me, but I used to live in Memphis when they made us sit upstairs in those buzzard seats....You're the one who got them to change that.' That was the first time I saw Sputnik with tears in his eyes."

Tears didn't fill the eyes of white Memphis teenagers, except perhaps when they laughed hysterically, but many of them were equally devoted to Sputnik. It was not uncommon to see white boys walking around with a white streak dyed in their hair. Samuel Joseph Behr had one, and when he died unexpectedly in a traffic accident, he was remembered for many things, including "his tremendous interest in Sputnik Monroe." As historian Robert Gordon wrote, "By bonding himself to the tension of the era, Sputnik Monroe became a hero to the rebellious white youth culture." Even Randy Haspel, a Billy Wicks fan, couldn't resist Sputnik's charms. Haspel formed Randy and the Radiants, one of the city's most popular garage bands during the 1960s. One evening, his band was playing at Club Clearpool when the owner ended their set early. As is often the case in Memphis, an argument led to violence, with Haspel receiving a busted lip from one of the bouncers. When he got home, his parents called the police, and the men were arrested. Charged with assault and battery and malicious mischief, the three received heavy fines from the judge. The following weekend, Randy and the Radiants were scheduled to appear at Clearpool again. Haspel hired an armed guard to watch over them, but as it turned out, he could have saved his money. As they began to play, the front door opened and Sputnik Monroe, followed by Johnny Dark, smashed into the joint. Defiantly standing there, he pointed at the concession stand, where the bouncers slouched with hatred in their eyes. "I want to tell everybody, these boys are Sputnik's boys," he said, pointing at the band. "And if you mess with them, you're messing with Sputnik." If the bouncers planned for a repeat performance, it evaporated with the smell of fear, sweat and stale beer.

Billy Wicks's love of wrestling was also beginning to evaporate. The travel between bouts was hell; every week he would wrestle in Memphis on Monday and then spend the rest of the week grappling in Pensacola, Mobile and Panama City. Saturday mornings, he was back in Memphis for TV, then he'd wrestle in Jonesboro, Arkansas, that night. However, as 1960 began, he wasn't quite ready to give it all up. He briefly became Sputnik's tag team partner, but the storyline changed again when Wicks agreed to put up his belt in another match with Sputnik. Monroe won the match to regain the state championship, but something far greater had been lost. The Sputnik/Wicks feud was over, and a glorious chapter in Memphis wrestling history ended. In October, Wicks met Gorgeous George at the Auditorium in what became his last great match. The Gorgeous One continued his pre-match antics, and when the bell rang, he was able to win the first fall with a brutal leg stomp to Billy's throat. Wicks came back with a series of drop kicks that won him the second fall and the decision. Fans did not yet know that Wicks had given his notice; he would soon report for duty as a deputy with the Shelby County Sheriff's Department. Over the next decade, he would pick up occasional matches, but his days as a full-time professional wrestler had come to an end.

Sputnik, however, wasn't about to give up. He was Tennessee champion, and the crowds still loved and hated him in equal measure. However, he really needed someone to fill his old rival's shoes. On a Monday night in March 1961, the Fabulous Jackie Fargo was in the middle of a match with Cowboy Lester Welch when Sputnik leaped into the ring and began spouting challenges to several wrestlers. Fargo was furious, and the two exchanged words before Sputnik exited the arena. To make matters worse for Fargo, Sputnik's interruption threw off his timing, leading to his defeat. A grudge match was scheduled for a week later to settle the score. Sputnik won the first fall with a body press, and Fargo countered with a back breaker to secure the second fall. Then things turned brutal. They whaled on each other so much that they ended up outside the ring, where the fight continued. It became so ugly that wrestling commissioner Tony Lawo stopped the bout and declared it a draw. Their next meeting was just as savage. Sputnik was bleeding so heavily from several large cuts above his right eye that the referee stopped the match and declared Fargo the winner.

With ticket sales among Black fans increasing due to Sputnik's popularity and his rebellion against segregation, promoter Buddy Fuller and his bosses, Gulas and Welch, began to think of ways to satisfy African American citizens' hunger for the mat game. In the early days, Black Memphians were forbidden from attending some wrestling matches, but when the Auditorium opened in 1925, a small, segregated section was opened for them. There were African American wrestlers performing in other parts of the nation, but not in Memphis. This changed on November 23, 1959, when Fuller added two Black women wrestlers, Babs Wingo and Mary Scott, to the Monday night card. For years, Memphis officials had been concerned that the sight of Black people engaged in violence, even the controlled environment of the mat game, would enrage white people and lead to a riot. No such incident took place during or after the Wingo/Scott bout, so Fuller booked two male Black wrestlers the following summer. Jim Mitchell had been wrestling since the 1920s and had become one of the most successful African American wrestlers in the United States. He was one of many grapplers who adopted the name "Black Panther," and it was by that moniker that he defeated Bill Williams at the first Black male wrestling bout in Memphis history. Babs Wingo returned to the Bluff City in 1962, where she was defeated by Ramona Isabelle, and Sweet Georgia Brown, touted as "no. 1 among the Negro girl wrestlers," was disqualified in her match with Dinah Beamon. For the first few years, exhibiting Black wrestlers was little more than a gimmick, but in 1965, Black wrestlers were slowly being integrated into the Memphis mat scene.

Sailor Art Thomas was the most popular Black athlete to wrestle in Memphis during the 1960s.

The most popular Black athlete to wrestle in Memphis during the 1960s was Sailor Art Thomas. Blessed with a powerful physique, Thomas became a devoted weightlifter after a stint in the navy, where he served in a construction battalion. After a few years of participating in bodybuilding competitions, Thomas entered the mat game, where he quickly became a prominent wrestler. He first came to Memphis in September 1965, where he was defeated by Tojo Yamamoto. In November, he joined with another Black wrestler, Prince Pullins. Unlike before, Thomas and Pullins were not restricted to wrestling other African Americans but instead were allowed to grapple with Yamamoto and Alex Perez. During the match, Tojo threw salt in Thomas's eyes, and the two clobbered Pullins, which led to him and Perez being disqualified. Not satisfied with winning by disqualification, Thomas and Pullins demanded a rematch, which was scheduled for the following Monday. It was their turn to be disqualified when the prince drop-kicked the referee in the face. The following year, African Americans gained even more acceptance when the Sailor was pitted against the NWA heavyweight champion Gene Kiniski. Thomas was able to gain one fall, but the champ pinned him twice to win the match and retain his title. When Art Thomas was given a shot at the NWA belt, Black wrestlers were fully integrated into the Memphis mat game, and more of them became a part of the weekly bouts. These included Matt Jewell, Luther Lindsay (who was a tag team partner of Mario Galento) and the Sundown Kid.

The man who threw salt in Sailor Art Thomas's eyes was one of the most popular wrestlers in Memphis during the postwar years. Harold Watanabe was born in Hawaii and began wrestling in the early 1950s under the moniker P.Y. Chung. However, hoping to tap into the remnants of hostility that Americans felt for their World War II enemy, he took his name from two architects of the Imperial Japanese war effort, General and Prime Minister Hideki Tojo and Admiral Isoroku Yamamoto. Arriving in Memphis in the summer of 1963, he quickly established himself as one of the city's most exciting heels. In his first bout, he fell to Tex Riley. Then he partnered with Hiro Matsuda to defeat the Bavarian Boys. At the end of the year, he teamed up with the Russian Ivan Malenkov to battle tag partners Jackie Fargo and Mario Milano. Tojo and the Russian won the first fall and the Fargo team the second. However, Malenkov was so beaten up that he could not reenter the ring. This forced the referee to award the match to Fargo and Milano, who went on to capture the Southern Heavyweight Championship. This set up a classic feud where the All-American hero Jackie Fargo and his partner Mario Milano defended their title and honor from the sneaky Nipponese Tojo Yamamoto and his traitorous new partner, Alex Perez. Their first meeting of 1964 was so brutal that the referee was forced to declare a no contest for "unnecessary roughness." The feud moved into its second phase one week later when Tojo and Perez beat Fargo and Milano to capture the southern tag team belt. The following week, team Tojo secured their title when they

Tojo Yamamoto mentored Jerry Jarrett, and the two were a famous tag team in the late 1960s and early 1970s.

clobbered Karl and Skull Von Stroheim. The feud reached its zenith when Fargo and his new partner, Don Fargo, wrested the belt from Tojo and Perez. When the conflict between Fargo and Tojo cooled, Yamamoto and Perez snatched the World Tag Team Wrestling Championship from Karl and Kurt Von Brauner.

Around the time Tojo began making his mark in Memphis wrestling, former NWA heavyweight champion Lou Thesz returned to the Bluff City to battle Pat O'Conner for the title. Unfortunately for the fans, neither Lou nor O'Conner was able to secure a fall, forcing the match to end as a draw. During 1962, Thesz racked up several victories in the Bluff City, culminating in a tag team match with Jackie Fargo against the southern tag team champs the Medics. The scientific wrestling practiced by Thesz, combined with Fargo's slow-walking strut and rough-and-tumble tactics, easily defeated the Medics, but the champs were disqualified after they knocked out the referee and then broke his substitute's nose. NWA rules stated that in the event of a disqualification, title belts would not change hands, so Thesz and Fargo were left with an empty victory. It will be remembered that Lou Thesz despised the Nature Boy Buddy Rogers, who in 1961 wrested the heavyweight championship from Pat O'Conner. In early 1963, he was given an opportunity to prove once and for all that scientific wrestling was more powerful than Roger's showmanship. The two met in Toronto, where Thesz used all his knowledge to easily dispatch the Nature Boy and capture the NWA heavyweight belt.

In the audience that night was a young man named Wayde Bowles from Nova Scotia, who soaked up everything Thesz and the Nature Boy did. One month later, Lou came back to Memphis to defend his title from a Russian named Nikita Mulkovich. The match carried with it a bit of the Cold War rivalry that existed between the United States and the Soviet Union when Mulkovich vowed to bring the NWA belt to the Communist world. In the end it was an empty boast, for Thesz easily whipped the Russian and kept the heavyweight title on the free side of the Iron Curtain. The belt remained in his possession for several years; Thesz successfully pushed back challenges from Dick the Bruiser, former heavyweight champ Pat O'Conner and Karl Von Brauner, and he teamed up with Jackie Fargo, defeating Professor Ito and Tojo Yamamoto. Thesz may not have been a sensational wrestler like Sputnik Monroe and Buddy Rogers, but he knew he was a star and acted like it. According to wrestler Buddy Wayne, Thesz "normally stayed at the Peabody, which was the nicest hotel in town at the time. If he couldn't get a room there, he'd stay at the Claridge. Most of the guys would walk two or three blocks, carrying a suitcase to the Claridge. Not Lou. He called a cab, drove those two or three blocks. And when he walked in, he had a suit on, or a coat and tie, and people just stood there and looked at him in awe. He was the champion; there was no question about it."

Meanwhile, Sputnik Monroe was attempting, and mostly failing, to break into other territories. Then his wife left him. Sputnik watched helplessly as his career and family slipped through his fingers. In hopes of easing his suffering, Sputnik turned to strong drink, which did little to help his career or life. However, he knew where he was still loved. Returning to Memphis often, he basked in the glory that was still within reach. In February 1964, Memphis gave Sputnik a shot at the NWA heavyweight belt when he was matched against Lou Thesz. Sputnik gained one fall and then Thesz captured the second. In the final stage of the match, Sputnik pulled one of his bad boy moves and was disqualified. The champ granted Sputnik a rematch for the following week, where he easily defeated Monroe with two falls out of three. In May, Sputnik met a new wrestling sensation, Sam Steamboat of Hawaii, in a title match for the Tennessee championship belt. Sputnik's losing streak continued when Steamboat captured the title and a new Cadillac promised to the winner. Sputnik was able to defeat Tojo, and he partnered with Buddy Fuller to crush Professor Ito and Yamamoto during a tag team event. In 1967, he established a new team with Lester Welch to crush the mysterious Blue Infernos. In their first bout, the Blue Infernos defeated Sputnik and Welch, but they came to feel their loss was due to the referee's bias toward the Infernos. So, a second match took place the following week. To ratchet up the heat, the parties agreed that a three-man tag team would take place between Sputnik and Welch on the one side and the Blue Infernos with referee Don Arnold on the other. Despite the obvious disadvantage, the three-person team was stomped into defeat by Sputnik and Welch. Monroe would collect many more victories, but the fascination Memphians had for Sputnik was dissipating as the 1960s ended.

Jackie Fargo and Tojo Yamamoto replaced Sputnik in the eyes of Memphis wrestling fans. Fargo's roughness appealed to Memphians, who cheered when he strutted in the ring. For example, Fargo agreed to a handicap match with Karl Von Brauner and Saul Weingeroff that required him to fight both men without the aid of a partner. The two beat the hell out of Fargo, who then joined forces with Don Fargo in a rematch two weeks later. It did not go well for the two supposed brothers, who were disqualified and lost the match. Whenever he suffered a string of defeats, Fargo would begin talking in an ominous fashion—"Can you hear it? Do you know what's happenin'? The gate is swingin' open. It's swingin' open. They haven't oiled it and it's rusty. That's right. That's right. I ain't gonna tell you who's on the way. But they're letting him out." He was referring to his real brother, Sonny "Roughhouse" Fargo, who supposedly would leave the North Carolina State

Jackie Fargo, seen here with his brother Roughhouse Fargo, was a legendary Memphis wrestler who dominated the mat game in the 1960s and early 1970s.

Mental Hospital to help his sibling out of a jam. Roughhouse's skills in the ring were not developed enough to prevent a victory for Von Brauner and Weingeroff, but it was a wild storyline that kept the fans longing for more. Jackie Fargo loved nothing more than a grudge match, and one of the best occurred in July and August 1967. A six-man tag team bout with Fargo,

Corsica Joe and Herb Welch versus the Blue Infernos and Oki Yamaha was so violent that the referee ended the match and refused to name a winner. Of course, this inconclusive decision brought more intensity to the rematch held the following week. This time it was a Texas Tornado bout that, like a battle royal, allowed all members of the team to fight in the ring at the same time. Six grapplers entered the ring, and after a terrific free-for-all, Fargo and his partners were left standing. Fargo also joined forces with Lou Thesz, winning the Southern Tag Team Championship in 1968. While Fargo was climbing the ladder of Memphis wrestling, he was also developing business interests outside of the mat game. He partnered with country and rockabilly musician Eddie Bond in establishing the Southern Frontier restaurant, which specialized in Fargo Burgers, as well as a sign-making company.

Tojo Yamamoto knew only wrestling, and he devoted himself to being a top attraction in Memphis. Tojo's villainy sometimes caused fans to forget themselves and become violent. One night, Tojo and Johnny Long fell to Jackie and Roughhouse, but the crowd was not satisfied with simply seeing them defeated. Flashlight batteries and other objects were chunked at Tojo and Long as they left the ring. Fans crowded the aisles, pushing and shoving the two wrestlers, who started swinging wooden sandals and handcuffs at anyone nearby. One was twenty-seven-year-old Tom Barnes, who was minding his own business when he received cuts to his back and wrist. He swore out a warrant against Tojo and Long, who were arrested and fined fifty dollars each for disorderly conduct. A few weeks later, forty-three year-old Edd W. Jones entered the ring during a match and cut Tojo with a pocketknife. In another sensational match, Tojo defeated twelve fellow wrestlers in a thirteen-man Battle Royal.

During the late 1960s, Tojo took under his wing a young man named Jerry Jarrett, who was born in Nashville and began hanging out at wrestling events at a young age. His mother, Christine, worked as a ticket taker for Gulas and Welch, and young Jerry sold programs at the age of five; by his teenage years, he was promoting small wrestling gigs in the Nashville area. Wishing to become a wrestler himself, he convinced Tojo to give him the training he needed to succeed in the ring. Once he learned the ropes, Jarrett partnered with Tojo in a series of matches against the southern tag team champions the Internes, which ended with their capture of the title. When Jarrett became older, he started booking matches and running promotions.

Jerry Jarrett was not the only young man in the late 1960s longing to enter the wrestling business. In Memphis, a young artist named Jerry Lawler spent a great deal of his time drawing caricatures of Sputnik Monroe, Billy

Wicks, Jackie Fargo and Tojo Yamamoto. Mustering his courage, Lawler sent some of his drawings to WHBQ-TV, where the main announcer of studio wrestling, Lance Russell, showed them on the air. It was exciting to have his art shown on TV, but what Lawler really wanted was to be a professional wrestler. Not knowing what to do, he called Billy Wicks on the phone and asked how one becomes a grappler. Wicks, impressed with the young man's sincerity, showed him a few techniques and urged him to get in touch with Jackie Fargo and Nick Gulas. At first, Fargo was more interested in his artistic skills; he and Bond hired him to work at their sign company, but the Fabulous One did introduce him to Gulas and Roy Welch. Eventually, he secured a disc jockey slot at Eddie Bond's radio station KWEM, which taught him how to connect with an audience and what it took to keep their attention. In 1970, Gulas booked Lawler for a match with Tojo Yamamoto in Jonesboro, Arkansas. It was a preliminary match, but it gave Lawler his start. No one knew it at the time, but these two young men, Jerry Jarrett and Jerry Lawler, would revolutionize the mat game and make Memphis the most creative and unconventional wrestling city in the United States.

Chapter 6

"WRESTLING FANS ARE THE FORGOTTEN MASSES"

1972–1980

Sputnik Monroe returned to Memphis in the early 1970s a dejected man. Many territories didn't want him, and even wrestling fans in the Bluff City no longer cheered as before. One evening, Randy Haspel, the young man Monroe protected from a beating at Clearpool, was hanging out at Sam Phillip's recording studio when Sputnik shuffled in. Lamenting that he no longer could generate heat with the fans, he said, "I don't know what to do anymore....I can't get these people to hate me like they used to!" Haspel suggested he tap into the hippie culture that was despised by many. "If you talked about love, Sputnik, they'd probably hate you." Sitting nearby was drummer Skip Owsley, who suggested Monroe find a Black wrestler to partner with. Norvell Austin eagerly joined Sputnik, and within a short time they were the most sensational act in Memphis. Their first appearance on studio wrestling was a watershed moment in the local mat game. To be sure, Black and white wrestlers had teamed up before, but no one acted as Sputnik and Austin did. In their first appearance on TV, Sputnik took a bucket of black paint and poured it on his opponent, ending the match. Then they went to the announcer's microphone. "Black is beautiful," Sputnik shouted. "White is beautiful," replied Austin. Sputnik grabbed Austin's hand, held their arms up and both shouted in unison, "Black and white together is beautiful!" Their performance signaled a new style in the TV show—more spontaneous and violent. As the decade progressed, the show became more and more wild and occasionally veered into the surreal.

Sputnik Monroe returned to Memphis in the early 1970s.

The television show also continued to increase attendance at the Monday night matches—so much so that the downtown Auditorium could no longer accommodate the fans. Fortunately, a few years before, the city had constructed the Mid-South Coliseum at the Fairgrounds between Central and Southern Avenues. The Coliseum could hold more people and was centrally located, and the parking was free. For the next twenty-five years, it was the home of Memphis wrestling. With such increased violence on Saturday mornings, fans naturally wanted to see more spectacular action on Monday nights. Jerry Jarrett wanted nothing more than to give it to them. He continued to partner with Tojo until Jackie Fargo took his place after their manager, Sir Clements, busted Yamamoto in the head with an umbrella during a match with the Von Brauners. A few weeks later, Tojo welcomed him back to the fold when he, Jarrett and Fargo walloped the Von Brauners and their manager, Saul Weingeroff. Two months later, Fargo dropped Tojo as his partner and joined with Jarrett. These shifting alliances increased fan excitement and were becoming in the early 1970s a hallmark of Memphis wrestling. Jarrett also briefly partnered with Lou Thesz to defeat the Bounty Hunters in front of 6,637 fans. In addition, Jarrett was booking matches for Gulas/Welch in Memphis and throughout the rest of the Memphis end of the territory. As the booker, Jarrett had complete autonomy, and he eventually signed a contract that he believed gave him 50 percent of the company.

While in Huntsville, Alabama, Jarrett watched Jerry Lawler wrestle and afterward approached him in the dressing room. Jarrett tried to share a few pointers just as Tojo and Fargo had done for him. Lawler was having none of it. "Really?" Lawler asked. "I'll tell you what. You wrestle your way, and I'll wrestle mine." Alabama had recently been added to the Gulas/Welch territory, and they sent young wrestlers like Lawler there to hone their skills and prepare them for Memphis. Insulting the booker was not a good way of advancing a career, but Lawler gave his all and soon became very popular in the North Alabama region. He was paired with Steve Kyle, and the two performed as the Lawler Brothers. It was there that Lawler met Sam Bass,

Left: Norvell Austin teamed with Sputnik Monroe in the early 1970s.

Right: Plowboy Frazier sided with Jerry Jarrett during his fight for the Memphis territory.

an experienced wrestler and manager who soon became a mentor to the Memphis native. Lawler's charisma and gift for ad-libbing were on full display in Alabama, and within a year he was brought back to Memphis, where he quickly became a staple of Saturday morning at WHBQ-TV and the Coliseum on Monday nights. He was partnered with Jim White, and the two secured the southern tag team title from Fargo and Jarrett in early 1973. Jarrett and Lawler may have gotten off on the wrong foot in Alabama, but as Jarrett became more and more responsible for creating storylines to promote the matches, the two worked closely together. Jarrett recognized Lawler's charisma and ability to work a crowd, while Lawler understood Jarrett's promotional brilliance. One of their first major promotions came when Bass and Lawler began working with the six-ten, four-hundred-pound Stan Frazier. Calling him Plowboy, they concocted an elaborate plot that intrigued the audience for many weeks.

The Plowboy was introduced as Bass and Lawler's servant who carried their bags, drove them to events and took care of their other needs. He was a kind of hillbilly version of Gorgeous George's valet, Jeffries. During their TV appearances, the audience learned that Bass and Lawler didn't pay Frazier with money but instead gave him a new diamond ring every week. One Saturday morning, Jarrett asked the Plowboy about his rings. "They tell me they're worth thousands." Jarrett then pulled out a hammer. Diamonds are the hardest substance on Earth, Jarrett said. "So, hitting it with a hammer won't do anything." Frazier agreed, and Jarrett reared back and hit the ring, which was blasted into smithereens. The audience howled when the Plowboy promised revenge, which he got many times with his new partner, Jerry Jarrett. The promotion also gave Lawler an opportunity to hone his skill ad-libbing insults and threats. He attacked Plowboy as an uneducated redneck from Mississippi at every turn. As the Plowboy storyline wound down, action again centered on Lawler and White's defense of their NWA southern tag team belt. Fargo and Jarrett hoped to snatch the title back from them, but when they wrestled for it on Saturday morning, Jarrett was injured, and the bout was canceled. Two days later, Jarrett had recovered enough for the four to battle it out for the championship. More than ten thousand fans, which was becoming the norm for Monday nights, watched as Fargo and Jarrett smashed Lawler and White to recapture the tag team belt. For the rematch, former heavyweight boxing champion Jersey Joe Walcott was hired to referee and keep order during the bout. In an upset, Lawler and White seized the tag team title away from their rivals.

One Saturday morning, Fargo and Lawler were trading insults and threats as they promoted their upcoming Monday night bout. "You know, Fargo, you've been the king around Memphis for a long time, but you're looking at the kid who's going to knock you off your throne." When Lawler defeated Fargo, the audience began calling him the king, and it stuck. He joined forces with Lou Thesz in crushing Roughhouse Fargo and Tommy Gilbert and then pulverized Gilbert for the NWA junior heavyweight belt. Fargo tried to take the title from Lawler, but the king successfully beat him back. In the late summer of 1974, the NWA junior heavyweight championship was renamed the southern heavyweight title, and Lawler captured the new belt when he smashed Robert Fuller in September. Two weeks later, NWA world heavyweight champion Jack Brisco faced him in a title match. According to Lawler, "I pulled out a chain where the referee couldn't see it for the finish. I used the chain on Jack and put it under my arm and covered Jack, one-two-three. People went crazy. I grabbed the belt, and the referee came over to raise my arm as champion. He took the wrong arm and as he lifted it up, the chain fell out and he reversed the decision." His popularity was such that Monday nights at the Coliseum averaged 9,500 attendees, and when the heat was on, attendance rose to a sell-out 11,000. Being such a box office draw as well as the southern heavyweight champion solidified Lawler's position

Jackie Fargo was a vital mentor to Jerry Lawler.

as the King of Memphis Wrestling. By the end of the year, he had made $90,000, which is roughly $477,000 in twenty-first-century money.

Like Jarrett, Lawler was always looking for new and unusual ways to promote local wrestling matches. In early 1973, he learned that Adam West, star of TV's *Batman*, was scheduled to be in Memphis at a custom car show. He arranged for West to appear on studio wrestling to promote the car show, not to mention Lawler's position as the territory's most popular heel. That Saturday morning, Lawler picked West up at his hotel, and the two ate breakfast before going to WHBQ-TV's studio on Highland Avenue. Dressed in his bat-cowl and a track suit, West was interviewed by Dave Brown, who mentioned his appearance at the car show before the actor explained the real reason for being in Memphis. "There is a rumor that Mr. Freeze and Penguin are here in Memphis because of the radical change in the weather and that they have a hook-up with the evil king of Memphis who just might be wrestling here this morning." Then Lawler walks in front of the camera wearing a Superman costume with a crown where the letter "S" should be. "Is that who I think it is?" West asks Brown. "Yes, it is," replied the announcer, who then asked Lawler, "What is this?" "Well, what does it look like?…I heard he was going to be here today, so I dressed appropriately." With Lawler describing himself as "Super-King," the two argued a bit before West said, "I don't think it's too late for you. I think that possibly, if you changed some of your habits, some of your methods of wrestling, if you'd use your left and right turn indicator in your car. Did other things that people normally do when they are polite and courteous and you weren't such a naughty, mean person, it wouldn't be too late for you." Super-King replied, "And I can see that you're not familiar with these rednecks that we have around here." Catcalls and jeers erupted from the audience, who were then defended by West. "These are splendid people. They are Bat-Fans, I know they are. I think it is insulting to call them rednecks." It is hard to imagine that such a strange spectacle could have happened in any other town. The creativity and downright weirdness of that brief promotion were signatures of Memphis wrestling during the 1970s.

One month after Lawler won the southern heavyweight belt, the *Commercial Appeal*'s Walter Dawson wrote an in-depth article about the King—the first major newspaper coverage of a professional wrestler since Kid Marley punched Sputnik Monroe in 1960. "He's one of those rare people that you meet with 'star quality' written all over them....He's not really a star wrestler per se; he's a star that happens to have gone into wrestling," wrote Dawson. In hopes of being a bigger star, Lawler recorded a song called "Bad News" at Ardent Studios and produced by the noted Jim Dickinson. Like Sputnik Monroe, you never knew what Lawler might do. Lance Russell became Lawler's foil during TV broadcasts. He frequently insulted Russell; his most recognizable was calling him "banana-nose," which soon entered the city's everyday language. One Saturday morning, Lawler and Sam Bass attacked Russell and tore clothing from his body. Lawler still hoped to become the NWA world heavyweight champion but was defeated by Jack Brisco in February 1975. However, he remained southern heavyweight champion when he met the Mongolian Stomper in July. A controversy arose during that match when referee Paul Morton ruled that the Stomper won, while ring announcer Lance Russell insisted that Lawler was the winner. National Wrestling Alliance President Sam Muchnick demanded a return match to discover who deserved the southern belt. About 11,500 fans packed the Coliseum to watch. Unfortunately for the Lawler fans in the crowd, the Mongolian Stomper defeated the King and tore the southern heavyweight belt from his grip. As the King worked to recapture his title, he squared off against a new wrestler named Bill Dundee. Born in Scotland and raised in Australia, William Cruickshanks was a circus trapeze artist who turned to professional wrestling. He immigrated to the United Sates and began wrestling in Memphis in 1975. Dundee tore Lawler up to capture the match, thus beginning one of the greatest friendships/rivalries in Memphis wrestling history. It would take Lawler until December before he recaptured the southern heavyweight title and further solidified his position as the king of Memphis wrestling.

During the early summer of 1976, the King was being interviewed on Saturday morning TV when he lamented that he had conquered the best grapplers in the mat game and was looking for a new challenge, declaring that he would meet in the ring any boxers or martial artists willing to take him on. The following Saturday, Rocky Johnson, a Black professional wrestler who claimed to be a boxer, appeared at the studio and agreed to meet Lawler in the ring. The match promised to decide who was the better athlete, a boxer or a wrestler, and it included a mixture of boxing and wrestling rules. The afternoon of the bout, Johnson and Lawler participated in a weighing-in ceremony where both men were interviewed by Charlie B. Watson of WHBQ Eyewitness News. Johnson stated, "I think I'm bigger than he is, I'm stronger than he is, and I know one thing, I can hit harder than he can." The King boasted, "I'm gonna prove a point once and for all, the question been going around a long time, who could win between a boxer and a wrestler. I'm gonna make everybody realize that there's no athlete in the world that can compare with a wrestler."

During the fifteen-round contest, Johnson seemed to be winning when Lawler cheated and was declared the winner. A rematch followed in July where more than ten thousand fans watched as Johnson knocked the King out in the sixth round. We should take a moment to consider the significance of this promotion. African Americans had been wrestling whites for barely a decade, and only four years had passed since Sputnik Monroe enraged white fans by declaring, "Black is beautiful." In 1966, Sailor Art Thomas was unable to defeat the white NWA champ Gene Kiniski, but in 1976, an African American grappler crushed the most popular white wrestler in Memphis. A Canadian, Johnson was born Wayde Bowles in Nova Scotia and moved to Toronto as a teenager. Hanging around at the gym, he got to know boxers, wrestlers and promoters who taught him the ropes and helped him go pro in 1962. When he joined the Memphis territory, Johnson experienced the casual racism that permeated the American South. When Nick Gulas disparaged him, he planted his feet and said in a firm tone, "My name is Rocky, not boy."

Rocky Johnson was the first African American to become the NWA southern heavyweight champion.

On July 26, 1976, three weeks after Johnson's victory, Lawler successfully beat back challenger Harley Race to retain the southern belt. When the bout was over, Lawler's manager, Sam Bass, peeled out of the Coliseum parking lot headed for Nashville. At mile marker 163, Bass plowed into a stalled car and was then hit by a tractor trailer that pushed Bass's vehicle into a ditch, where it burst into flames. Bass and his passengers, Pepe Lopez and Frank Hester, died instantly. Lawler was devastated. Sam Bass had been his best friend and the mentor who transformed him into the King of Memphis Wrestling. But there was little time for grieving. More bouts were scheduled, and he had to make regular TV appearances. The most important match was a title bout with NWA world heavyweight champion Terry Funk. Lawler endured a ferocious sixty-minute battle with Funk where he gained nothing more than a draw. Also, he was needed by Jarrett for a new promotion/storyline where a stable of wrestlers called "Lawler's Army" were led by "General" Jerry Lawler. Dressed in an army surplus uniform equipped with real medals and a helmet, the King directed his charges, cheated when he could and riled up the audience with his obnoxious behavior. However, veterans and their organizations resented seeing Lawler wearing a uniform he had no right to, bedecked with commendations he didn't earn. During the Lawler's Army controversy, the King put up his southern title in a rematch with Rocky Johnson. The former boxer told fans that he wanted to take on the King so bad that he would abandon his boxing career and become a professional wrestler. The crowd at the Mid-South Coliseum was delighted to watch Johnson pound Lawler into submission and take his title from him. Lawler refused to hand over the belt and stormed out of the ring. However, it didn't matter. Rocky Johnson had become the first Black NWA southern heavyweight champion.

Christmas Day 1976 fell on a Saturday, and instead of canceling the weekly TV show, WHBQ broadcast a special holiday edition of studio wrestling. The program included Christmas-themed interviews with many of the most popular wrestlers. Tojo Yamamoto explained, "Since I came to the United States, and I wrestled in Memphis, and they backed me up a hundred percent 'til the time I came to Memphis and now I want to wish… all Memphis wrestling fans a Merry, Merry Christmas and a Happy New Year." A film crew visited Rocky Johnson's home, where he introduced his wife, Ata, and his four-year-old son, Dwayne, who was called Dewey by his family. During the interview, anxious young Dewey wanted desperately to open a Christmas present. Jackie Fargo offered his holiday wishes for everyone—"except you Lawler, bah, humbug!" The King was shown writing a letter to Santa Claus asking for a new wrestling partner. After he finished his correspondence, Lawler fell asleep, and when he awoke, a

Nick Gulas, seen here with his son George, ran the Memphis territory from 1957 to 1977.

big package was sitting by his tree. Opening it, he was surprised to find a man dressed in a gorilla suit, who carried him away. The broadcast ended with Nick Gulas wishing everyone a Merry Christmas and "a prosperous new year." The aging promoter didn't know it, but his new year would be anything but prosperous.

When 1977 began, Nick Gulas and Roy Welch owned a large territory divided in two. The Memphis end included Evansville, Indiana; Jonesboro, Arkansas; Lexington and Louisville, Kentucky; and Tupelo, Mississippi, while the Birmingham end consisted of Chattanooga; Huntsville, Alabama; and Nashville. Jerry Jarrett ran the Memphis end, which was very profitable due to Jerry Lawler and the wild promotions that kept fans hungry for more. According to Jarrett, the Birmingham end was not profitable at all. Gulas refused to engage in storylines and promotions and spent most of his time trying to build his son George into a major star. Welch believed that Gulas wanted to destroy the Memphis end, but he wouldn't stand for it. It was too profitable, and Welch knew how to run a successful operation. Plus, he liked and respected Jarrett. Unfortunately, Gulas did not. To make matters worse, Welch was terribly ill and was no longer able to make the necessary decisions to keep the business running. It was only a matter of time before Gulas made a stupid decision that would jeopardize the territory. It came in March 1977.

One day, Jarrett was in the Nashville office he shared with Gulas and his team. Nick stuck his head in and said very matter-of-factly, "I'm sending George to the Memphis end next week. He has been on the Birmingham end too long." He wanted Lawler to be sent back to Alabama and make his son George the top wrestler in Memphis. Jarrett knew that this wouldn't work. He replied that he would never agree to exchange his biggest money maker for his son. "Have you forgotten that I own 50% of this business and you can't tell me who to book?" When he started making matches for Gulas-Welch in 1967, Jarrett began buying shares in the company, which totaled $50,000 by 1977. In an ominous tone, Gulas told him to contact their attorney, Cecil Bramsetter. Jarrett realized that he had been shafted when Bramsetter informed him that he had only signed an option to buy the business—and it had run out the day before. Storming into Gulas's office, Jarrett calmly declared, "You are making the mistake of your life. You and your crooked attorney are not bright enough to understand that regardless of what I do, you can't make money in the towns you promote, and a change in towns will not change your inability to make money." After talking with his wife and mother, Jarrett decided that he would quit and start his own promotion. In his resignation letter, Jarrett stressed that he did not own any part of the business and was not a partner. It was obvious that he needed the King if he was to have a successful business, so he reached out to Lawler. The two agreed to a partnership in the new venture. Bill Dundee, Plowboy Frazier and several other grapplers joined Jarrett and Lawler, and they recruited Buddy Fuller, Roy Welch's son, to be a minority stakeholder in the new enterprise. The promotion was named the Continental Wrestling Association, an affiliate of the NWA, which was owned by the Jarrett-Welch Wrestling Company.

As we have seen, television was of vital importance to the mat business. The new partners met with Lance Russell and Dave Brown in the hopes they would host a new show sponsored by them. However, the owners of the station got wind of the situation and, fearing a lawsuit, canceled studio wrestling. When fans heard the news, it was like a bomb going off in the middle of a match. Lance Russell, program director of WHBQ-TV, had hosted the show since 1960 and Dave Brown since 1967. For many fans, they were as important to the mat game as any wrestler. Jarrett was able to negotiate a new show on WMC-TV, but Russell and Brown were trapped by their respective contracts. Or at least that's what they said. The truth was that both men were making plans to leave WHBQ and join WMC, but the details had yet to be worked out. The fans didn't know this, and so the fate of Lance and Dave became a storyline and generated its own kind of heat. For example, thirteen-year-old Kevin Jones was rather upset: "It's going to seem funny without Lance to commentate. Nobody can do it like Lance. All my life I've watched him, since I was real little." Jerry Lawler played along, saying, "My only problem will be getting used to an announcer without a big nose." The first WMC wrestling show was broadcast on March 19, 1977, with Clay Conrad announcing. As the first broadcast was ending, Jarrett's heart sank when he saw that Fargo and Tojo did not show up for the taping. The night before, both had reassured him of their loyalty, but now it was clear they were siding with Gulas. What he did not know, and wouldn't find out until 2011, was that Fargo believed Jarrett was trying to steal Gulas's entire territory and told him so. Setting up the new company was ultimately easier because many in the wrestling business trusted Jarrett and distrusted Gulas. As wrestler Bob Armstrong explained, "I had no problem working for Jerry Jarrett. Before Jarrett's split with Gulas, I

Jerry Lawler being interviewed by Lance Russell.

had agreed to come into Memphis and work against Lawler and I had no problem following through with my commitment as long as Jerry needed me. He paid me very well and it was a pleasure to work for him."

Although he lost the TV show, Gulas still had a contract with the Mid-South Coliseum for Monday night wrestling. This forced Jarrett to find an alternative night and venue for his new promotions. The newly renovated Auditorium, now called the Cook Convention Center, was available, so Jarrett and Lawler held their first matches the day after their television debut, Sunday, March 20; 8,256 braved downtown Memphis to see Lawler meet Bob Armstrong in a stretcher match without a referee, which resulted in both men being carried out of the ring. In the other significant match, Rocky Johnson held on to his southern heavyweight belt against Plowboy Frazier. The following night, Monday, March 21, saw the debut of the new Gulas card. A mere 2,000 people attended the matches at the Coliseum to see Bobo Brazil, George Gulas and Tojo Yamamoto. In addition to being a better businessman than Gulas, Jarrett was a better storyteller. "My style of producing wrestling was to try to emulate life," Jarrett later said. Despite this early success, Jarrett needed the support of the National Wrestling Alliance if he was to stay in Memphis. When the board of directors met in April, he and Gulas were there to plead their cases.

The demeanor of the two men could not have been more different when they appeared before the board. Gulas was angry, demanding that Jarrett be kicked out of the NWA and Memphis be given back to him. In a calm, measured way, Jarrett responded that he didn't want revenge against Gulas, that he had tried to work with him, but it became impossible. Let both companies compete in Memphis, Jarrett suggested, and the better product would prevail. Jarrett's reasonable behavior, his lack of animosity and the support of Roy Welch's son convinced the board to allow both men to operate in Memphis. This was a disaster for Gulas. Ticket sales were anemic, and his Birmingham territory was also in jeopardy. Gulas didn't have enough money to rent the Coliseum for a few weeks in April, which gave Jarrett an opportunity to temporarily use the Coliseum on Sunday, April 24. Rocky Johnson, who had lost the southern title to Lawler a few weeks before, lost to NWA world heavyweight champion Harley Race, while Lawler smashed former NWA champ Jack Brisco with the help of a small bag of powder that temporarily blinded the ex-champion. The April 24 card was a huge success for Jarrett; 8,693 fans came to see his show, while Gulas was averaging only 2,000 for his Coliseum events. The day before, Lance Russell made his debut on WMC Channel 5 wrestling. He had retired from

WHBQ and now worked for Jarrett's company. During that first broadcast, he and Lawler made the most of it. "You've wallowed in obscurity ever since we left that other station and you couldn't stand it. Somebody tried to tell these people you've been fishing and hunting. You've been sitting glued in front of that television to Channel 5 watching me out here making a bigger star out of myself and you're realizing that the people are forgetting about you and that's why you're here today," Lawler taunted. Russell came back with, "One of the hesitations I had in coming back here was the fact that I was gonna have to listen to that mouth that hadn't gotten any smaller." Dave Brown joined WMC-TV in May and was again by Lance Russell's side.

Jarrett was able to book one more Sunday night card at the Coliseum on May 1 where another 8,000 fans attended. The next night, only 1,474 attended Gulas's matches, and one week later, on May 9, only 484 people showed up. That was the end of the line for Nick Gulas. He would never again offer a wrestling card in Memphis. He ran Nashville promotions for several years with Fargo and Tojo, but he eventually sold what was left of his mat empire to Jarrett and went to work for the Davidson County Sheriff's Department. Despite his hard-nosed reputation, many of the wrestlers had good things to say about him. Bill Dundee, for example, stated, "Nick never treated me bad. There were plenty enough times I did something or another and he would have been justified in doing so, but he didn't." Even Lawler had nothing negative to say about him. "You know, a lot of people knock Nick, but I actually got along great with the guy.…He was OK in my book and treated me well."

By the end of May 1977, the Gulas-Jarrett war was over, and wrestling had settled into its old routine. Monday night wrestling at the Coliseum was back, and the only real difference is that you had to change your TV dial from channel 13 to channel 5 on Saturday morning. The switch had been very successful for WMC—it was now the number one station in Memphis, and Dave Brown was the city's most popular weatherman. Lawler kept his southern heavyweight belt by defeating Paul Orndorff, and Rocky Johnson, who was now known as "Soul Man," crushed David Schultz. Fighting a rookie like Schultz was something of a come down for the former southern heavyweight champ. As popular as he was, there wasn't a great deal of room at the top while Lawler ruled the scene. So, Johnson decided it was time to leave the Memphis territory to work in other places—but not before he met Lawler one last time. Advertised as a "special challenge match," the two squared off against each other until Lawler secured the win. Meanwhile,

Bill "Superstar" Dundee began wrestling in Memphis in 1975.

Jarrett began a new storyline with Bill Dundee, who was now calling himself "Superstar." He faced Lawler protégé Bad Bad Leroy Brown, who beat Superstar senseless during a Saturday morning broadcast. Unable to wrestle on Monday night, Dundee appeared the following Saturday morning, where he vowed to destroy Leroy Brown. Lawler then ridiculed the Superstar's chances, calling him a sawed-off runt. Enraged fans flocked to the Coliseum the following Monday night to see Dundee take on the Bad One. The Superstar seemed hopelessly outmuscled until he jumped off the second rope and pinned Brown with a flying body press. The fans loved it, and Jarrett spread it out for a few more weeks. When it was finished, Dundee was the giant-killer, and Lawler wanted to get his hands on the punk who defeated his man. This was the perfect setup for one of the greatest wrestling feuds in Memphis history.

The temperature in Memphis reached ninety-seven degrees on the Fourth of July 1977, but the heat was stronger inside the Coliseum. For the match between Lawler and Dundee to take place, each man had to put up $3,000, and the King agreed to pin the Superstar two times within fifteen minutes or lose his money. At the end of the allotted time, Dundee had not been pinned and therefore became $3,000 richer. Recently, Dundee had bought a new Cadillac, and when Jarrett saw it, he had an idea. For the next bout, he announced that the car belonged to Lawler, and he put it up beside the Superstar's $4,000. The time limit and number of pins were the same, but this time both men were put inside a cage. Dundee prevented the two pins and walked away with the new Cadillac he already owned. The feud was now two weeks old when Lawler fought Paul Orndorff and recaptured his southern heavyweight belt. At the end of July, the King put up his title and the Superstar his Cadillac for a fight to the finish. Lawler again fell to the giant-killer, and Bill Dundee was crowned the NWA's southern heavyweight champion. Jarrett turned the heat up even further in August when the King put up his hair against Dundee's Cadillac. This time the Superstar came up short, and Lawler took the title and the car. The two met in another title match where the Superstar put up *his* hair and the King put up the belt, Cadillac and his manager Mickey Poole's hair. Dundee prevailed—Lawler lost the title and car, while his manager had his head shaved in the center of the ring. At the end of August, the two met in a Texas Death Match, which had few rules—the winner was the last man standing on his own two feet. By that time, fans had been whipped into a frenzy, and the feud was the talk of Memphis. Everyone wondered what would happen next. In the August 29 match, the King regained the title and the Cadillac, but what would happen in September?

"There comes a time when you have to sit down and take a look at what you're doing," Lawler explained to the press. He had been thinking about the death of Elvis Presley, which had taken place a few weeks before. Life was short, Lawler thought, and he wanted to concentrate on his artistic and musical careers. In July, he released a record titled "The Ballad of Jerry Lawler," which contained such lyrics as "I can sing better than Johnny Cash. I am greater than Muhammad Ali. I am prettier than Farrah Fawcett." No one who heard that record could possibly believe he had a future in the music business, but it didn't matter. It was all part of the game. Time seemed to stand still for wrestling fans when the King announced that he was retiring from the mat game. Some hated to see him go, while others couldn't wait to show him the door. He and Dundee met on September 5 for what was supposed to be the King's final night. The match culminated in Lawler defeating the Superstar, who had his hair shaved off because of his defeat; 10,129 fans bought tickets for the bout, which made Jarrett think he could have one more match between the King and Superstar.

The following Saturday morning, Lawler appeared on TV to say goodbye to his fans. As he spoke to Lance Russell, he started ragging on Dundee and his wife, Beverly. "The pressure on Dundee was so bad that he was thinkin' about wakin' up lookin' like a cueball in the mornin.' Ya know, I told you about his old lady, this old hag he keeps home up in Nashville. She told him, she said, 'Bill Dundee, let me tell you somethin,' don't you come home if you lose that hair cause I don't never want to see that ugly face with no hair on it.'" Then, out of nowhere, a woman rushed Lawler and started slapping him. As he pulled away from her, the Superstar appeared from backstage, grabbed the woman and walked her to the back. Above the excited noise of the audience, Lawler pointed and squealed, "That's Dundee's old lady right there, look at that! Look at that fool! That is the greatest thing I've seen in my life! Dundee brought his old lady down here to fight his fight for him! Did you rednecks see that?" You could barely hear Lawler as the crowd jeered and laughed at him. The Superstar came out and demanded a rematch to settle the King's beef with his wife, but Lawler refused. However, when Dundee slinked away, Lawler called him back and said he'd give him the rematch if Dundee put his wife's hair up. He didn't want to, but the Superstar said yes; his agreement set up the final bout in the Dundee/Lawler feud of 1977. Fans had no idea what would happen next, but nine thousand of them came to the Coliseum to find out. The King ended up prevailing over the Superstar, and Beverly Dundee bravely walked into the ring and had her head shaved. Much of the crowd was angry, and the Superstar thought for a moment that the fans would rush the ring. So did the seventy-year-old barber who was quaking in his shoes as he cut her hair. Despite the humiliation, the Dundee family were pleased with the result. Husband and wife each got $3,000, and the Superstar was now a household name in Memphis. "My haircut money was the down payment on our new house. With Beverly's haircut money, we were able to fully furnish our house with new furniture. Until my hair grew back it was hard to look in the mirror every morning, but it sure felt good to wake up in the new bed inside our house," Dundee remembered.

With Lawler out of the game, a round-robin tournament was held to choose the new southern heavyweight champion. Jack Brisco, Leroy Brown, Bill Dundee, Bruce Swaze, Mr. Wrestling and a newcomer to Memphis, Handsome Jimmy Valiant, participated in the series of matches. The Superstar faced Handsome Jimmy in an opening bout designed to introduce the rookie to the Memphis crowd. Dundee was supposed to win the match, but the crowd was so excited by the Handsome One that Jarrett sent word for the match to end in a draw; Valiant would advance into the tournament on a coin toss. In the final round, Handsome Jimmy defeated Mr. Wrestling and was crowned the new southern heavyweight champ. As we have seen, Lawler was ostensibly focusing on his musical career, which led him and his backing band, Jimmy Hart and The Gentrys, being invited to perform at Monday night wrestling before the main event featuring Handsome Jimmy and King Cobra. As the band played, Valiant walked on stage and smashed a guitar upside Lawler's skull. As Lawler stood there bleeding and writhing in pain, something happened to the fans. For five years, the King had been the city's greatest heel—taunting the audience, cheating fellow wrestlers and otherwise reveling in villainy. The crowds loved it, but he was still a bad man. However, when Valiant hit him over the head, something began to change.

The following Saturday morning, Lance Russell showed a video of Handsome Jimmy telling fans that he would no longer wrestle in Memphis after Monday night because they didn't deserve to see a wrestler as talented as him. Lance, Dave and the audience were wondering who could possibly stand up against Valiant, and then the phone rang. Lawler was on the other end, and he asked to be patched into the broadcast. The King explained that he was enjoying his retirement and wanted only to make music, but if they wanted him back, he would meet Handsome Jimmy on Monday night. Everyone, including the studio audience whom Lawler frequently called "rednecks," wanted him back to face the newest heel in town. The King smashed Handsome Jimmy from one end of the ring to the other when they met at the Coliseum. Valiant couldn't keep up, and Lawler earned the victory and the southern heavyweight belt. Lawler's transformation into a baby-face hero was complete a few weeks later when the Superstar and Norvell Austin were wrestling Dennis Condry and Phil Hickerson on studio wrestling. Running from the back, Handsome Jimmy bolted into the ring and attacked Dundee and Austin. As fans screamed, Lawler strutted between the ropes and began pounding Valiant to win the match for the Superstar. As Handsome Jimmy and his allies slinked away, Dundee offered the King his hand, and he took it. Lawler was now a hero and was partnered with the most popular baby-face in Memphis.

The Lawler/Handsome Jimmy storyline continued to dominate the local mat game. At the end of the year, the King was given another pass at the NWA world title when he met Harley Race at the Coliseum. As the King moved to pin Race, Handsome Jimmy entered the ring with a bottle in his hand. Valiant busted the bottle over Lawler's head and then stabbed him in the chest. Lawler fell into the broken glass lying on the mat and had to be taken to the hospital. The King suffered severe cuts on his shoulder and arm, a fractured finger and several cuts on the head. The NWA banned Handsome Jimmy from Memphis, but Lawler wanted a return match, so he circulated a petition on Monday night for Valiant to be reinstated. The King's ploy worked; Handsome Jimmy was reinstated, and the two battled in early January 1978, where Lawler was defeated after the referee reversed his decision and gave the match to Handsome Jimmy. According to Lawler, "Everyone talked about Handsome Jimmy, the boy from New York City. That was his theme song. Then he started calling himself 'Handsome Jimbo from Mempho.' Other people started calling Memphis 'Mempho.' He called me Kingfish and people started doing that, too." In 1978, Jimmy released a song called "Rock and Roller," which was nearly as boastful as "The Ballad of Jerry Lawler." "I came rollin' into Mempho, TWA. Tell all the ladies Handsome Jimmy's on his way. I'm a rocker and a roller, a little funky, too."

Meanwhile, the Superstar and the King continued their partnership, and in the fall of 1978, they defeated the Bounty Hunters for the southern tag team championship. The following Saturday morning, Lawler and Dundee were discussing their plans for a rematch, which included a stipulation that Bounty Hunters manager Chuck Malone put up his hair. As the King finished explaining the upcoming bout, Valiant walked in front of the camera. "I got a hell of an idea, baby! You know Handsome Jimmy, the hottest thing, baby, in the world, baby.…Everyone wants to pay to see Handsome Jimmy and what I want right now, I wanna talk to the Kingfish…and I want to talk to the Superstar. Can you imagine, Handsome Jimmy, Superstar, and the Kingfish in the same ring and in the same time, with, Baby, Chuck Malone and the Bounty Hunters? What do you think about that, huh?" Lawler and Dundee didn't think too much of the idea and tried to explain that a six-man tag team bout was not possible for Monday night because it was a title match and they wanted Malone bald. "You know what, Kingfish, I think I feel a little jealousy here. "I think I feel—." Dundee tried to interrupt, and Valiant replied, referring to the Superstar's five-foot-seven frame: "Hey, shortwind, go play with some short people." Then the temperature started to rise. "What the problem is, you're on a preliminary match. Do you know what a preliminary match is? That's where the promoters put preliminary wrestlers, that's where you are," the King explained. "Let me tell you the whole thing right now. I know exactly what it is, daddy. You are jealous of Handsome's body, daddy. You are jealous of my old lady, daddy. You are jealous of my record.… You're a sick man. You're very sick, baby." "Let me tell you somethin' Handsome Jimmy," Lawler stated with a finger pointed in Valiant's face. "I'm not jealous of you, because let me tell you just exactly what you are.…" Jerry Jarrett and promoter Eddie Marlin then walked on stage to restore order. "No, you guys don't have to come out here. We'll settle this right now. It ain't no way I'm gonna be jealous of a big fag-lookin' jerk like you [homophobic slurs were still in use during the 1970s]. You got bleach-blonde hair, you got those long goofy handlebar mustache, you got a tattoo painted on that queer ear of yours, and you got one fingernail painted silver, now what's that for?" The two continued to argue and point fingers until Lawler slapped Jimmy in that handsome face of his. Jarett and a group of wrestlers surrounded the King, while others restrained Handsome from smashing a chair over Lawler's head. A few weeks later, Valiant got a tag team match with his partner Wayne Farris against the King and Superstar, who easily defeated Handsome Jimmy and his protégé.

As we have seen, Jerry Lawler transitioned from being a heel to a babyface in 1977, and by 1979, he was bigger than either of those categories. Both hero and villain—everyone in Memphis knew, and many followed his exploits. No one, not even Jim Londos or Sputnik Monroe, had ever been a bigger personality in Memphis wrestling. In the summer of 1979, Lawler wrestled an up-and-comer named Jimmy Golden. In the crowd that night was *Commercial Appeal* reporter Greg Haney. He watched Lawler nearly get pulverized before coming back at the last minute for the win and spoke with many of the fans. Seventy-three-year-old Lily Baker, wearing a "Jerry Lawler is King" cap, explained that she watched outdoor matches on Main Street when she was a little girl and saw the action at the Lyric Theater and the Auditorium before following wrestling to the Coliseum. He also interviewed Huxley King, who explained that Memphis wrestling is "more entertainment than sport. Ninety percent of the people root for the good guys, but I cheer for the bad guys. What's it all about? Aggression. You let go of your inhibitions. You can come out here and watch somebody get their head dusted off. It's a show." Despite Lawler's popularity and the brilliant storylines, the CWA was in trouble. Jarrett's booker, Robert Fuller, Buddy Fuller's son, took most of Jarrett's talent to the Knoxville territory, leaving Lawler, Dundee and a few others behind. The promotions had become rather stale, and the fans stopped coming. Average attendance at the Monday night bouts dipped to four thousand. Jarrett needed something big and soon.

Meanwhile, southern tag team champs Dundee and Lawler were locked in a bitter feud with the Blond Bombers Wayne Farris and Larry Latham. The four were scheduled to meet at the Tupelo, Mississippi sports arena on June 17, 1979. In planning the match, Jarrett wanted the match to spill over outside the ring so Lance Russell could film a brawl up close like no one had seen before. The Tupelo fans were solidly behind Dundee and Lawler and had every reason to believe they would hang on to their belts. Dundee pinned Farris twice, but referee Jerry Calhoun was outside the ring trying to stop Lawler from beating on Latham. Calhoun was also roughed up, and when he reentered the ring in a daze, he saw Farris pin Dundee; he groggily awarded the title to the Blond Bombers. The fans were furious, and so were the King and Superstar. Long after the bell had rung, they beat the Bombers to a bloody pulp, but they continued to struggle. The fight poured into the aisles, and then the lobby, and smashed into the concession stand. Russell had indeed noticed what was going on, and he followed the action with his cameraman. "Hey, Mike, can you get the camera? They've got a hell of a fight going on down here." Once filming began, Russell, reminiscent of the *Hindenburg* disaster radio broadcast, described the scene:

> *What you're looking at is the wildest fight we've seen. Latham and Farris and Dundee and Lawler in the concession stand. All four of 'em bleeding; pounding each other. Lawler, oooh, fired a gallon jug. They're bangin' away. Watch out Mike! Dundee with Latham and Lawler with Farris. Oh, there's mustard all over us! I hope it didn't get the camera. Referee tryin' to get 'em stopped. Dundee right on top of Latham right below us. We're on the stairs leading down to the concession stand. What a brawl! I've never seen anything like it. They're trying to get somebody to help stop this thing. This is just totally out of hand. Latham and Farris, Lawler and Dundee in the concession stand at the Tupelo Sports Arena brawling all over the concession stand. A gallon bottle has been thrown, glass on the floor. Lawler slams Farris with a stool and again. Lawler rattles a pan around. Dundee on the far side bein' stomped on the concrete, can you get it? with Latham. In 27 years of it I've never seen a battle like this, and Lawler, tryin' to be strangled by Farris while Dundee with a mop wailing Latham. Promoter Jerry Jarrett, although he is not a promoter here, tryin' to get 'em to stop. He's got Dundee separated. Lawler. Latham, having been racked up by that mop handle, Dundee goin' after him. It's just a street brawl. Jerry Jarrett with referee Jerry Calhoun. Jarrett trying to get it all stopped. Dundee picks up a table. Everything broken up. They're falling all over. Mustard everywhere! Farris laying in the middle of the floor. Dundee rushed outta there.*

Lance Russell wasn't the only one shocked by the concession stand brawl. Nearly the entire city of Memphis watched the footage on Saturday morning and were talking about it over the next few weeks. The next Monday was a sellout, and the renewed interest gave Jarrett the leverage to bring new talent into Memphis. The most important wrestler Jarrett brought to Memphis in the summer of 1979 was Terry "the Hulk" Boulder. Described as being "the most awesome figure in professional wrestling today," whose "measurements are almost unbelievable," fans couldn't wait to see him in person. Tommy Davis, a fan from Byhalia, Mississippi, said, "We saw the Hulk on television and wanted to come see if he was as big as he looks." He teamed with his "brother," Eddie Boulder, to defeat Ron Bass and Pete Austin and then was smashed by Bass in a single bout. Attendance steadily increased during the summer. On August 6, 7,549 people watched Farris and Latham defeat the

Superstar and Rick Morton and the "Hulk" team up with Jackie Fargo to stomp Bass and Sonny King. At the end of the month, Dundee captured the southern heavyweight belt from Ron Bass, and Boulder with Tommy Gilbert smashed into Farris and Latham to win the match by disqualification. While Jarrett was rebuilding his audience, Lawler recruited his friend and lead singer of The Gentrys, Jimmy Hart, to be his new manager. Hart was at the King's side when he retained his southern heavyweight title against Paul Orndorff and was his tag team partner in their victory over Ken Lucas and Steve Regal.

In the fall of 1979, a film crew from NBC television arrived in Memphis to do a story on wrestling for its *Prime-Time Sunday* program hosted by Tom Snyder. Broadcast two days before Christmas, the show focused most of its attention on the Bluff City. Snyder explained as the camera focused on the ring, "This is Memphis, where Monday night wrestling is an institution. Where you will find Mary Spry, front row, red blouse, silver whistle every Monday night." "I love my wrestling more than anything. In fact, I'd rather go up there than any place I ever been in my life. I don't go out honky-tonkin', don't drink. I shoot the pinball machine once in a while, but I'd give that up if I had to," Spry explained. Then she stated, "They say I'm crazy to go up there and say it's silly because it's all fake and all this stuff, that's fine with me." There was a whiff of condescension in the report's emphasis on violence and fakery. Lawler was filmed saying, "I'm gonna go through Handsome Jimmy just like Ex-Lax through a widow woman!" Mrs. Spry stated, "The more violent they get, the better I like it." However, Jarrett took the opportunity to set them straight when he proudly declared, "The wrestling fans are the forgotten masses.…They are very much middle America." The so-called elite may not have liked the image of Memphis presented by the national media, but the show solidified the Bluff City as the most innovative and significant wrestling town in the United States.

In early February 1980, Lawler was playing football with a group of friends, including Jerry Calhoun. He had just purchased a new set of cleats, and the ground was wet when he ran the ball up the field. Lawler explained, "My cleats stuck when I put all my weight on the right leg. The old bone went, and you could hear it crack all over the field." In fact, Lawler's leg break was heard all over Memphis; hospital phones were jammed with fans trying to get in touch with the King, while the local media extensively covered the story. Furious didn't even begin to describe how Jarrett felt. Telling Lawler, "The territory is built around you. You're not just a wrestler; you make the profits and here you are trying to re-live a lost childhood playing football with other wanna-be athletes. And now here the top star that we have everything built around, is gone."

What was going to happen to the business now that its star attraction was unavailable for at least six months? No one in Memphis knew the answer as spring slowly made its way to the Bluff City.

Chapter 7

"WE'LL ALWAYS HAVE WRESTLING"

1980-2024

As we have seen, Jimmy Hart had recently been named Jerry Lawler's manager. With Lawler temporarily out of the picture, Hart developed a persona that set the city on fire. His basic approach was to be as obnoxious as possible. "No matter what happens to me if I'm always real, feisty, real colorful and just laugh all the time. If somebody come to you and calls you whatever you want to, if you just laugh in their face and go, it's like oh God, I'll kill him." Jarrett later explained that "Jimmy brought a vibrant energy to our territory because he's so high and hyper instinctive and he carried that to television, and he carried it to the ring."

Jarrett was working on a strategy to keep the territory going when he realized that Jimmy Hart and his "vibrant energy" were the key to the whole promotion. On the Saturday after the King's accident, Hart appeared on studio wrestling, dressed in a white tuxedo and carrying a crown. Everyone assumed that Lawler's manager would be encouraging and sympathetic to his fallen star. Lance Russell set the interview up by reminding the audience that Hart was a confidant and "cheerleader" for the veteran grappler. We want "to find out from Jerry's closest friend the conditions of Jerry Lawler and his broken leg." Then Jimmy Hart opened his mouth. "Are you finally through? Are you through? It's right, Jerry Lawler broke his leg, big deal, man! You know who broke his leg? I'm tellin' everyone, Jerry Calhoun, baby! He broke the man's leg. But listen, I don't want to talk about that anymore. Let me ask you somethin' Man. If you have a prize racehorse, a thoroughbred, a champion, and he breaks his leg. What do you do to him? What do you do to him, Lance! You shoot him, right? Jerry Lawler is no good to me anymore.

He can't make me anymore money, baby! The future is now. He's on you. So, listen. Don't ever talk about him in front of me again. You understand that?" Hart then introduced his newest find, the Iranian Assassin. Dressed in a red keffiyeh and robe, the bearded wrestler looked a bit like some of the imams then holding Americans hostage in Tehran. Later in the broadcast, Hart introduced Paul Ellering as the "new king of wrestling," which didn't go over very well with either Russell or the audience. The southern heavyweight champ Handsome Jimmy Valiant didn't like it either. When Hart placed the crown on Ellering's head, Valiant walked on the floor and objected. "I don't know what you're on, but high or straight, you know deep in your heart, Jimmy Hart, that I am the real king of wrestling!" Hart used a bit of persuasion on Handsome Jimmy to temporarily give Ellering the crown, but a few weeks later, Valiant crushed Ellering to retain his southern belt. No matter how hard Ellering and Handsome Jimmy tried to wear the crown, there was only one King of Memphis wrestling and everyone knew it. As the months dragged on and Lawler and Hart continued to snipe at each other, everyone wondered, when would the King return?

Jimmy Hart began as Jerry Lawler's manager and then became head of the anti-Lawler First Family.

In the spring of 1980, Hart renamed his stable of wrestlers the First Family, whose main goal was to pulverize Lawler and knock him off his throne. Meanwhile, the King was champing at the bit to get back in the ring. He visited the TV studio several times, but by the end of the summer, he could wait no longer. After two surgeries and seven months of therapy, Lawler believed that he was ready to return. Of course, everyone wanted him to face Jimmy Hart to punish him for the racehorse comment, and 7,604 of them had the privilege of watching the King beat him to a pulp. Unfortunately, it was way too soon for Lawler to be in the ring. He tore up his leg some more and had to stay off it until after Christmas. On December 13, Lawler appeared on the Saturday morning show to inform Lance Russell and the fans that he was cleared to perform at the end of the year. As Lawler described his plans to force Hart out of the mat game, the president of the First Family climbed into the ring and taunted the King. "I tell you what, Lance, this is too good to be true," said Lawler as he rolled into the ring and punched Hart in the face. They were soon joined by five members of the First Family, with one carrying a baseball bat. The King laid into them until surrounded by a vicious circle of Jimmy Hart's lapdogs. Then Lawler's cousin Carl Fergie plowed into the ring as the First Family scattered through the ropes.

The heat in the Coliseum reached tropical levels on December 29, 1980, when 11,069 fans witnessed Lawler's return to the ring. He wrestled twice that night. First, he walloped the newest member of the First Family, the Dream Machine, then he wanged Jimmy Hart in a revenge match. Unlike previous promotions, the storyline didn't end in a few weeks. For the next few years, nearly all of Lawler's matches were somehow connected to his feud with the First Family. Like a soap opera, the cast changed regularly, but the two leads, Lawler and Hart, remained the focus of the show. They also devised new gimmicks to keep things fresh. Hart lost his gold record of The Gentrys number one hit "Keep on Dancin'" when the King crushed Austin Idol, and Lawler was able to give Hart ten lashes with a whip after he defeated Ron Bass.

Membership in the First Family remained fluid as some wrestlers broke with Hart while others took their place. Hart brought in Terry Funk from Florida to wrestle Lawler in a special challenge match that became one of the most brutal and violent bouts Memphis had ever seen. Seven minutes into the match, the two men were pummeling each other mercilessly. They continued to pound each other with their fists until Lawler knocked him to the mat, jumped from the turnbuckle and landed hard on Funk. The cowardly Hart entered the ring and tried to thump the King with a chair. He dropped it as Lawler thwacked him in the face; then Funk picked it up and smashed the King's leg. Jerry Calhoun pulled the chair from Funk, who brutally racked Lawler's leg repeatedly with his fist and employed a spinning leg lock. Hart threw the chair back into the ring, but Lawler rolled away when Funk swung down on him. Nailed right in the face, Funk staggered as the King used the chair to knock him down. Lawler repeatedly bashed Funk's leg with the metal chair even after he rolled out of the ring and onto the concrete floor. As Funk lay unconscious, the King was able to reenter the ring and was declared the winner. Soon after his defeat, Funk issued a challenge to Lawler to meet him alone for a grudge match. The two met in an empty Mid-South Coliseum on the afternoon of Saturday, April 25, 1981, with only Lance Russell and cameraman Randy West there to record the event. When the two entered the ring, Russell provided the play-by-play. The two pounded each other with chairs and fists while Russell and West worked to record the melee. Funk caught Lawler in a piledriver and then ripped a two-by-four from the ring and tried to jam it in Lawler's eyes by its jagged edge. It looked as though the King was going to lose his eyesight and the match when Lawler kicked Funk's elbow, driving the club into Funk's left eye.

Then Terry Funk began to scream. "My eye! I can't see! Doctor! Doctor! God help me! Please help me!" For the next few weeks, Funk appeared on Saturday morning sporting an eye patch and raving about the "Empty Arena Match." "Sure, I'm missin' some teeth. Yes, I've got permanent damage to my eye, but have you seen Jerry Lawler?" Many saw the King at the end of May 1981, when he defeated Funk in twenty minutes and thirty-six seconds. The Empty Arena storyline and subsequent bouts between Lawler and Funk continued to draw large crowds and the TV show huge ratings. As Memphis wrestling historian Mark James explained, "This feud between Lawler and Funk was one of the most brutal and bloody the fans had ever seen to this point." In the summer of 1981, Gary R. Salles phoned *Commercial Appeal* entertainment reporter John Knott to complain about the lack of wrestling coverage in the newspaper. "Really, after all that isn't sports. That's entertainment," Knott declared. "Well," Salles replied, "the entertainment section doesn't cover it, either. Wrestling is more than sport. It is entertainment. Cheap, too. And right now, some of the top names in the world of wrestling are regularly at the Coliseum and its TV tie-in.... We wrestling fans are some of the most avid TV viewers in town. I think you'd be surprised how many of us have come out of the closet in the past few years." While Lawler was focusing on his feud with Terry Funk, the Dream Machine had secured the southern heavyweight belt, and Dirty Dutch Mantell held the Mid-America heavyweight championship. In November, Mantell creamed the Dream Machine and won the southern title. Lawler then challenged the dirty one for the southern belt, which the King easily won in early 1982. In mid-April, Lawler successfully teamed with Jackie Fargo in a match against the First Family's Dream Machine and the Monk. While Lawler, Funk, Mantell and the Dream Machine were going after each other, a nationally known TV star was dreaming of becoming a professional wrestler.

Andy Kaufman grew up in New York watching the World Wrestling Federation promotions, owned by Vince McMahon Sr., and he remained a fan as he became well known as a comedian and performance artist. In his standup routines, Kaufman would offer $1,000 to any woman who could defeat him in a wrestling match. There were many takers, but the comedian would always come out on top. In 1981, Kaufman was starring in the ABC-TV show *Taxi* and performing in clubs across the United States. Increasingly, he was adding more wrestling themes into his performance art, even going so far as to bill himself as the "World Inter-Gender Champion." He asked his friend Bill Apter, who published several wrestling magazines, to contact Vince McMahon Sr. for an opportunity to bring his "inter-gender" act to a professional setting. McMahon Sr. turned him down, so Apter contacted Lawler, who was interested in the promotion. Jarrett was brought into the discussions, and he remembered their first meeting. "His pitch was simple. He says, 'I'm Andy Kaufman and I love professional wrestling. I have been doing a routine in my club acts in which I wrestle women. The crowd loves it and now I'd like to wrestle in a real professional wrestling promotion.'"

In his first match in Memphis, Kaufman defeated three women, but during his second appearance on November 30, 1981, he nearly lost to a woman named Foxy. After the match, the Hollywood star sat down with Lance Russell for his first appearance on Saturday morning wrestling. "I've never met a woman in the three-and-a-half years that I've been doing this who was able to pin my shoulders to the ground," Kaufman explained. "Now I'm not saying that women are mentally inferior to men because when it comes to things like cooking and cleaning, washing the potatoes, scrubbing the carrots, raising the babies, mopping the floors, they have it all over men. I believe that, but when it comes to the wrestling, when it comes to them getting in the wrestling ring, there's nothing up there, they're all oatmeal north of the eyebrows. They're all Wheatena for brains, you know what I mean? I will pay $1,000, I'll take on anybody who wants to come in that ring and volunteer. I don't think you can do it. You know why? Cause I'm gonna send you back to the kitchen where you belong. I'm gonna have you scrubbin' the potatoes and washin' the carrots because that's where you belong, ladies."

Russell showed the tape of the Foxy match, and Kaufman provided his analysis of the bout. "At the beginning of that, if you look at it closely, you can see she was even taking advice from the great Jerry Lawler. Even the great Jerry Lawler with his advice, she still couldn't do it." As this monologue shows, Kaufman was brilliant at generating heat. Not even Jerry Lawler or Jimmy Hart was able to get under the skins of wrestlers and fans alike better than Andy Kaufman. The Hollywood star agreed to a rematch with Foxy, who had Lawler in her corner to offer advice and support. After pinning Foxy to the mat, Kaufman refused to let her up while pummeling her head. Lawler jumped into the ring, picked up Kaufman and threw him across the mat. The two tussled briefly before Lawler walked away. Lance Russell was on the floor with a microphone, which Kaufman used to great effect. "I will sue Lawler, I will sue you! You don't touch me; I am from Hollywood! I'll get Hollywood against you, baby! I'll sue you, baby! Lawler, I don't wrestle men, you don't touch me, baby! I'll sue you for everything you've got! You won't have anything left when I'm through with you!"

A few months later, Lawler was relaxing at home when he heard a knock at the door. A delivery man handed him a package that contained an alleged legal deposition and a videotape. The following Saturday, Lawler brought the package to the WMC-TV studio, which broadcast its contents:

> *Hello, Mr. Lawler, remember me, I'm Andy Kaufman from Hollywood. Remember you pushed me around in the ring the last time I was down in "Maymphus," Tennessee. Let me tell you something Mr. Lawler, I am not a hick. I am not from Maymfus, Tennessee, I don't come from Tennessee, like you do, OK? I come from Hollywood, California, where I make movies and TV shows. I am a national television star and I want the respect that I deserve when I come down to Memphis. I don't like any hick like you pushin' me around the ring. I never agreed to wrestle you, I was wrestling someone else. You stuck your nose in, you came in the ring, pushed me around, and you know what I'm going to do? Mr. Lawler, I have a lot of money, OK, a lot of money, and I've hired a lawyer and I'm gonna sue you for every cent that you've got, every cent that you're worth. You will be in*

> *debt to me for the rest of your life. You'll never eat again when I'm through with you. You'll wish you never heard the name Andy Kaufman; do you hear me?*

Lawler replied, "I've got a very simple solution for you, wimp....What I would propose, and what I think everybody would love to see is Andy Kaufman come and get in the ring with a real wrestler and let him see what it's like to really wrestle." Kaufman's schedule did not allow him to stay in Memphis long, so the videotaped messages he sent pushed the storyline forward and generated more and more heat.

"Hello, Mr. Lawler, I've heard all these things you been sayin' about me on television. You wanna wrassle me Maymphus style? Alright fine, I'm not afraid of you Mr. Lawler because let me tell you somethin', true I only wrestle women, but I've wrestled women a lot bigger and stronger than you. Matter of fact they're probably smarter than you cause you don't have any brains, you're from Maymphus, Tennessee. All ya do is plow the fields, and farm the farm. Is that how you talk in Maymphus, Tennessee, Mr. Lawler?... You challenged me to a wrestling match and I think you bit off a little more than you can chew. I'm gonna wipe the floor with ya, Mr. Lawler!" To prove his point, he grappled with a 327-pound woman. When it appeared that she was hurt, Kaufman yelled, "It doesn't matter. She doesn't have any money. She's poor, she can't sue me!" Lawler, simply replied, "You're gonna get hurt, son." Everyone in Memphis was talking about the Lawler/Kaufman feud. The Hollywood star was the most hated man in town, and had he walked down any street in the Bluff City during the months of March and April 1982, he would have been assaulted if not worse. Repugnance for Kaufman had the people by the throat, and almost no one was immune from its effects.

A police cordon surrounded Kaufman as he entered the ring at the Mid-South Coliseum on the evening of April 5, 1982. Lawler, dressed in his trademark crown and robe, soon followed. Noise from the crowd was deafening. "Kill him! Kill him!" one woman shouted. With both men in the ring, Lawler lunged for Kaufman, who quickly bolted through the ropes. This continued for several minutes. Each time the King tried to put his hands on Andy, he jumped out of the ring. Finally, in frustration, Lawler grabbed the public address microphone. "Let me ask you somethin'. Did you come down here to wrestle or act like an ass?" He reentered the ring and stood there with his hands behind his back, telling Kaufman, "I'll stand still, and you can get a headlock on me." After a few tentative moments, Andy did so, but then Lawler sprang his trap. He picked Andy up by the waist and slammed him with a side suplex. Andy laid there on the mat until the King picked him up and smashed his head and neck into the mat with a piledriver. Over the PA system, Lance Russell announced, "Jerry Lawler, six minutes, and fifty seconds with a piledriver, has been disqualified. The winner by disqualification is Andy Kaufman." Then Lawler did it a second time. The crowd didn't care. The man who ridiculed and laughed at them had been clobbered and now lay on the mat, unable to move. Paramedics entered the ring, put a neck brace on him, gently placed Andy on a stretcher and transported him to St. Francis Hospital. There was no sympathy in the crowd that night. Fans cheered, pointed and laughed at Kaufman. Mary Spry was there that night, full of brimstone for Kaufman. As he was being wheeled out of the Coliseum, she screamed, "That's tellin' 'em right, trash. Son of a bitch!" Another fan simply said, "Goodbye, Andy."

Diagnosed with a strained cervical spine, Kaufman was the talk of the town. The *Commercial Appeal* ran a big story, as did WMC's *Action News Five*. "Kaufman is in the intensive care unit at St. Francis Hospital," explained Jack Eaton. "He has had a battery of tests, and it is believed that he is not seriously injured." Once he was able, Andy agreed to an interview from his hospital bed. "I always thought wrestling wasn't real, but apparently, I guess at least this one was." When he was released from the hospital, Kaufman made another appearance at the Mid-South Coliseum wearing a neck brace. "OK, ladies and gentlemen, I'm leaving! And I'm never, never, coming back to Memphis again! You'll never see this face again!" The overjoyed crowd cheered loudly, but then Kaufman double-crossed them. "I shall return, my friends. I shall return. Shut up! Shut up!" The national media was also fascinated by this story. He appeared on ABC's *Good Morning America*, and in May he made another visit to *Saturday Night Live*. Speaking with Brian Doyle-Murray, Kaufman explained how he came to Memphis and offered commentary as the tape from the match was shown. In a defeated and serious tone, he apologized to the wrestling community for "making a mockery of the sport these past few years" and the women who he wrestled and "offended by saying those nasty things I've been saying." Then he asked for forgiveness. It was a brilliant move, and whether planned or not, it led directly to one of the greatest moments in American television history.

Kaufman's appearance on *Saturday Night Live* piqued the interest of a producer from *Late Night with David Letterman*, who invited him and Lawler to appear on the July 28 broadcast. When they arrived in New York, both men met with producer Robert Morton and sketched out how the appearance would go. The producer wanted the two to argue and threaten each other before the commercial break. When they came back, Andy would apologize for insulting the wrestling profession, and Lawler would apologize for hurting him. Then Kaufman would sing, "What the world needs now is love, sweet love." After the meeting, they went back to their hotel rooms, where Kaufman called Lawler and the two talked about how the apology would end their feud, possibly forever. Neither one liked it, but this is what the show wanted. Then Andy had an idea. "What would happen if I apologized but you wouldn't accept my apology and you slugged me?" Lawler laughed at the prospect but said, "Since the show is taped, if I slugged you and we didn't do what they asked us to do, one; they probably wouldn't air it. Two; they'd probably have me arrested." Kaufman agreed, but he asked the King to "just think about it."

That evening, Lawler walked on stage first to a chorus of boos. Then Kaufman, still in the neck brace, entered amid rousing cheers from the audience. Letterman asked Andy if he still needed the brace, and he explained that his neck was healing but the pain he endured still required support. Kaufman stated that he thought he could beat Lawler because he had defeated many women who were bigger than the King. Letterman asked Lawler if he ever doubted that he could crush Andy, and after saying no, he really cut loose. "I don't want to sit out here and pretend that I'm friends with this guy because I think he's a wimp. You see, I think when Andy was born, his father wanted a boy and his mother wanted a girl, and they were both satisfied." Kaufman sat there looking embarrassed as some of his insulting clips were screened. Then they went to commercial. When they returned, both men, through eye contact and subtle gesture, decided to go off the rails. "That's why I came here, because I asked for an apology. I apologized for all the wrestling I've ever done, all the abuse I've ever given. The people who didn't understand what I was doing, and I simply ask, think an apology is in order," said Andy. Letterman asked the King if he would apologize as well, and Lawler replied, "I don't think I owe him an apology. I think you know he says it was all a big joke." Letterman asked if the King wanted to hurt Kaufman, and he stated, "Yea, I thought I had to hurt him." Andy explained that in all his inter-gender matches, he never hurt someone. The back and forth generated a growing sense of menace in the air.

"You know, it's something that I take very seriously, it's the way I make my living, and he comes in making a joke out of it. He did it all for publicity, that's why he's still wearing—I don't know if it's a neck brace or a flea collar," Lawler quipped. "I had to spend three days in the hospital in traction, and I was given this neck brace in the hospital. It's a very real neck brace, it's a real thing….I just don't think there was any, it really wasn't called for. Dude, you could have, I could've been killed, and I could've had my neck broken," Kaufman detailed. Letterman pointed out that Andy did not have to go into the ring, to which Lawler replied, "That's right, I don't come out here and try to do standup comedy or anything like that. You know, I'm a wrestler, you're a comedian." Then Andy cranked it up. "If you were the man that you think that you are, then you'd apologize." Then they argued about the sportsmanship and their respective professions. "Well, I was going in the ring. It was something that I was doing, there was no need to hurt me." "As a joke, right?" "As a joke, yeah." "It's not a joke to me….Did you laugh when you were laying in the hospital, was it a joke then?" "There wasn't any reason to purposely hurt me, you could've proven the point by just beating me. You want to prove what a big man you are." Letterman rang a bell to stop the argument and then explained that many people think wrestling is a show, not an athletic contest, and asked if this was all simply a sham and the two were friends. The King denied it, and both men continued their verbal sparring. "That's exactly what he thought about wrestling. He thinks it's all a big joke, a big fix or whatever, and then you're right a lot of people that think that." Andy stated, "You're nothin' but a redneck, and you're just trying to prove a point because I was a Yankee, I heard this from so many people in Memphis." Lawler retorted, "There are a lot of people that think that, and he was one of them, and I did to Andy exactly what I would like to do to everybody who thinks that way. It was a chance to show him what it's really like, and he found out what it's really like."

Kaufman adjusted his body in the chair to sit at an angle toward Lawler. "Let me tell you something, my father said, my manager said, they all said I had a right, I could have gotten a lawyer, and I could have sued you for what you did. I didn't. All I want is an apology….I could have sued you for everything you're worth. Well, I didn't because I'm not that kind of a guy." Lawler stared closely into Kaufman's eyes and then asked, "What kind of a guy are you?" Kaufman pointed to Lawler as Letterman called for a commercial break. Lawler stood up. Kaufman looked him in the face and mumbled something. Suddenly, Lawler swung his right arm and slapped Kaufman on his left cheek, and Andy fell to the floor. This was not what David Letterman and his producer had in mind. Lawler was rushed into the back as Kaufman played it for all it was worth. When the commercial break ended, the King was back in his chair, and Kaufman was in a rage, wandering around the stage. "This is bullshit! You are full of bullshit, my friend! I will sue you for everything you have!" The expletives continued to fly as Andy played his part to perfection. "I will get you for this!" He stormed away but immediately returned. "I am sorry! I am sorry to use those words on television. I apologize, I'm sorry, I'm sorry, but you, you're a f*****g asshole!" Andy then threw a cup of coffee, and Lawler chased him off the set. The entire Confederate army couldn't do it, but Memphis culture had invaded the North, and its people were dumbstruck. NBC executives were deeply concerned about the legal ramifications and how the FCC would react. A network lawyer met with Lawler, Kaufman and producer Robert Morton. According to an NBC vice-president, "We satisfied ourselves that the producers of the show were not a party to planning or staging what happened in any way." On the other hand, Memphians were overjoyed. No doubt Mary Spry slept well that night. Kaufman went back to Hollywood to film the next season of *Taxi*, but the door was open for a continuation of the feud.

Counting the receipts from the Lawler/Kaufman feud, Jarrett was desperate to find someone as exciting and unpredictable as Andy Kaufman. While Jarrett was looking for his newest promotion, James Harris of Senatobia, Mississippi, returned home from a series of wrestling gigs in Europe and Japan, where he performed under the name Sugar Bear. His wrestling gear was on a boat steaming for America, so he drove to Memphis in search of new gear. He hoped to borrow some equipment from his friend Troy Graham, who wrestled under the name of the Dream Machine. While waiting, he ran into Jarrett and Lawler, who were already familiar with his Sugar Bear act. The two promoters asked him to wrestle for them and promised to develop an angle that would play to his strengths. They decided on a monster that wouldn't speak and wore distinctive body paint. Wanting to keep the white racist element of his audience and expand it if possible, Lawler and Jarrett created the character of Kimala the Ugandan Giant, a cannibal from Africa adorned with bright white and yellow paint. When they presented the concept to Harris, he thought, "What better kind of animalistic monster is there than a cannibalistic monster? One who wants to eat the enemy when he is done? A wrestler fighting this character would not only have to worry about being beaten, but he would also have to worry about being eaten."

Harris's first appearance as Kimala came in a promo video they shot for Saturday morning. He drove to Jarrett's Hendersonville farm, where Lawler painted his makeup, and they filmed him running around the woods, which stood in for the jungles of Uganda. With jungle drums beating in the background, the narrator intoned, "Kimala—six foot, nine inches tall.

Kimala—385 pounds. Kimala—the biggest man known to professional wrestling today....As strong as some of the largest animals known to man. Kimala—the Ugandan Giant!" When they finished filming, Jarrett asked, "So, James. I just want to make sure. You won't be ashamed to do the character on TV, right?" "I am not ashamed to do nothing. As long as it is going to make me money, too," he said. As far as Harris was concerned, he was acting a part, not playing into a racist fantasy, although he knew full well that many in the audience would be laughing at him. Kids who turned the channel from cartoons to watch studio wrestling were scared to death of what they saw, while adults wanted to see what he could do in the ring. Kimala made his debut at the Mid-South Coliseum on June 7. About 6,400 fans watched as Lawler went up against the Ugandan Giant to defend his southern heavyweight title. Lawler gazed at Kimala as if he were a wild animal, and the Ugandan sized the King up as a snack. Because the character was not supposed to know anything about wrestling, Kimala employed vicious chops to weaken his opponent. According to Harris, "About halfway through the match, I chopped the hell out of him and then just randomly jumped into the fans to see their reaction to the character." The chops worked, and Kimala became the new southern heavyweight champion. Through the summer of 1982, Kimala defeated Bill Dundee, Stever Keirn, Stan Lane and King Cobra while smashing Lawler several times. Kimala's reign ended on August 9 when 11,300 fans saw the King finally win over the Ugandan Giant.

Lawler and Jarrett were not racists, but they knew their audience. For many of them, they wanted nothing more than to see a Black wrestler get knocked out of his senses. They may not have liked their company, but they loved their money. There is no evidence that Sailor Art Thomas, Bobo Brazil, Koko Ware and Norvell Austin ever faced any overt racism, but we do know that Rocky Johnson did when he refused to accept being called "Boy." Sputnik Monroe's "Black is beautiful" promotion with Norvell Austin certainly played into racial feelings, and Lawler introduced an element of racism during the Plowboy Frazier storyline in 1976. During a Saturday morning show, Plowboy brought a watermelon that Lawler made Dave Brown eat. "We gonna eliminate the trash in professional wrestling," the King explained. Then he asked Frazier, "You remember a few years ago when you had a little trash problem down there in Philadelphia, Mississippi?" "Yea, I remember," the Plowboy replied. "What'd you do to it?" "Well, I got my bulldozer, and I put 'em underneath that pond down there in Philadelphia, down in Neshoba County." Lawler and Frazier were

Bobo Brazil mentored Kimala and was one of several critical Black wrestlers in Memphis.

referring to one of the most brutal crimes of the civil rights movement, when Freedom Summer organizers James Chaney, Andrew Goodman and Michael Schwerner were murdered in June 1964 in Neshoba County and buried under an earthen dam.

Ugly stuff, and it was tapped again when Kimala was in town. After Lawler defeated him, Kimala was recruited by Jimmy Hart to join the First Family. On Saturday morning, Hart debuted his newest member. "What Jimmy Hart wants, Jimmy Hart gets, man. You know what, I really realized the man was mistreated. Can you imagine, this man, Kimala, the Ugandan Giant, has never ever tasted a watermelon in his life. He didn't know what a watermelon tastes like, looks like—can you imagine depriving this child of that? Can you imagine, Kimala, has never even been with a woman in the United States? He hadn't even partied with any girls or anything, and you know the parties the First Family has. Russell, can you imagine a big watermelon party with Kimala and all those pretty little girls?...Watermelon and women, Kimala!" The Giant was scheduled to wrestle Dutch Mantell in the studio, but after Hart tried and failed to bring Mantell back into the

Kimala was one of Memphis's most popular Black wrestlers during the 1980s. He became a national figure when he changed his name to Kamala and joined the WWF.

First Family, he walked out, and Lawler agreed to take his place. "Let me just say a few words here to you Mr. Hart, you little, stinking, slimy wimp. And listen up! You can run all over the country and you can tell everybody that you won that belt for me, but you couldn't beat your way out of a wet paper bag, punk! I'm the one that beat that big Ubangi and I did it then and I can do it any day of the week, do you understand that?....I'm fixin' to take that big Black jerk and I'm gonna beat the paint off his face and then I'm gonna wet his lips and stick him to that wall right over there and then, Hart, then I'm gonna do the same thing to you!" According to Harris, they always told him what they were going to say beforehand, and if he was offended by any of it, they would take it out. Despite the racist overtones, Harris played Kimala brilliantly. When he was on TV, he walked the stage and approached screaming fans while seeming to be confused and about to lash out in frustration. Like Tojo Yamamoto, Jackie Fargo, Handsome Jimmy Valiant and Bill Dundee, Kimala is still one of the most beloved wrestlers to have ever worked in the Memphis mat game, even though he left Memphis for other territories, slightly changed his stage name to "Kamala" and later joined the WWF.

While the Kimala storyline was playing itself out, the National Wrestling Alliance's world heavyweight champion Ric "Nature Boy" Flair made a quick trip to Memphis, where he appeared on the Saturday morning show. "I want to admit to you, and I want to apologize to a lot of people out there. I've had the wrong impression of Memphis. You know, I got off my jet today, and they had a real big airport here. I even saw a couple Cadillacs on the highway as I came over here to the TV station. Contrary to my beliefs, from what I heard a real literate TV announcer and Memphis really is showing me a lot more class than I was led to believe....A person like myself, who obviously is a top-shelf individual, is led to believe that Memphis was nothing but rednecks and low-class people, and I'm really amazed." Adopting some of Andy Kaufman's language and combining it with a cool swagger, Flair had the fans wanting his head. The Nature

NWA world heavyweight champion Ric Flair battled Jerry Lawler on the Saturday morning TV show.

Boy then signed a contract agreeing to fight the southern heavyweight champ, who at that moment was Jerry Lawler. Flair was scheduled to wrestle an unknown named Ric McCord, but after the contract signing, Lawler goaded the NWA champ into wrestling him for ten minutes and putting his belt on the line. Just as the match was getting underway, Flair offered the King a way out. Speaking to Russell, he said, "Why don't you make that clear to the audience and make that clear to Lawler, if you want the easy way out, brother, just get out of the ring and I'll forget it." Lawler, of course, refused.

When the match ended without a fall, the King asked the champ for an additional five minutes, and Flair agreed. Lawler came on strong and was in the process of pinning Flair when the champ broke the hold and ran out of the ring. This seemingly left the title in limbo, and Lawler claimed it. However, the Nature Boy violently explained that there was no contract and therefore the match was not a title bout. Walking on camera with, wait for it, Jimmy Hart, Flair began screaming, "Just a minute, brother, where is the contract? Show me a contract that said I wrestled for the world championship?" Then Flair said between clinched teeth, "You will never see the day that I wrestle Jerry Lawler, and you know why? I'll tell you why. Get in here, big man!" Wrapping his arm around Hart, the Nature Boy yelled, "This seems to be the only man in the whole town that I can look in the eye and believe!…I flew my Lear jet in here out of the goodness of my heart, and you country bumpkins, you rednecks trying to put something over on Mr. Cool. No way, Daddy, not today." He then wrote a check for $10,000 as a bounty for Hart to bring him "the blood and the sweat and the guts of Jerry Lawler!" This should have led to a main event bout between Lawler and Flair, but it never happened. The two didn't meet in the Coliseum, and the promotion faded into the wind. The reason was that for years the NWA had made it known that it would never allow Lawler to become world heavyweight champ. It's not known why, but it was a fact. Jarrett and Lawler's inability to guide this promotion to its logical conclusion suggested that there was a problem somewhere that might threaten the long-term health of the territory. But first, the Hollywood star slunk back into Mempho.

In the spring of 1983, the TV series *Taxi* was canceled, leaving Andy Kaufman at loose ends. He appeared several times on *Late Night with David Letterman* and participated in a Rodney Dangerfield TV special, but in between he came back to his first love. In early May, he partnered with the Colossus of Death in a handicap piledriver match against Lawler. Kaufman tried to use a piledriver on the King, but he couldn't do it and Lawler won the bout. In a post-match interview with Lance Russell and Jimmy Hart, Andy was back to his old tricks. "You fans who started booing and hissing me tonight, don't try that again! Don't try that again! I am a star! The next time I come here I want you all to get down on your knees and bow down to me! If I pass you by, kiss my feet!" During the summer and fall of 1983, Part II of the Kaufman/Lawler feud played out at the Coliseum and on Saturday morning TV. The biggest match of the summer took place on July 4 between Lawler and the team of Kaufman and Hart. About 8,800 fans watched as the two wimps tried to wrestle the King. Each man stood in a corner and waited for Lawler to enter the center ring. At one point, Kaufman rushed him, and while Lawler was busy beating him, Hart jumped on his back and began choking the King with a chain. Lawler fell to the ground, and Kaufman and Hart kicked him several times. As Lawler writhed in pain, Hart picked him up and held his hands, and Kaufman slapped him in the face. Hart couldn't hold the King for long, but he took a couple of cheap shots as Kaufman danced around the ring. Then Hart made a terrible mistake. He hit Lawler on the back of the head, and the King went ballistic. Hart threw Kaufman into Lawler to help his escape, but the King punched Andy out of the way and grabbed Hart, who was smashed to the mat. Both challengers writhed on the canvas as Lawler stood there triumphant. When referee Jerry Calhoun tried to stop him, Lawler used a piledriver on Kaufman and then did the same for Hart. Lawler was, of course, disqualified, but neither he nor the audience cared. Then the Bruise Brothers, Porkchop Cash and the Dream Machine pummeled the King before Austin Idol entered the ring and swatted them through the ropes.

The following Saturday, Kaufman made his in-studio debut on Championship Wrestling. Back in the neck brace, Andy offered $10,000 for any wrestler who could put Lawler in the hospital. The crowd started chanting "We Want Hart," as Kaufman turned on his erstwhile partner. "Jimmy Hart talks me into doing this…he says nothin' gonna happen, Andy. Nothin's gonna happen. He gets me in the ring with Lawler. Monday night we get in the ring, and he runs out, he's chicken! I'm gonna take on

The Andy Kaufman–Jerry Lawler Feud was among the greatest in Memphis wrestling history and garnered national media attention.

Hart. I know I'm gonna beat that guy.…If he was here right now, I'd beat him. I'd beat him right now if he was here!" Then Hart walks out. The two argued over who was more responsible for the defeat until Kaufman slapped Hart, who returned the favor. Lance Russell tried to break it up and was soon joined by promoter Eddie Marlin and Dave Brown, who separated the two. Andy ran to the ring and gestured for Hart to join him. Grabbing the microphone, Hart hysterically screamed, "You slapped me in front of 350,000 people out here. Nobody slaps me in my hometown!" The two withdrew backstage, but Kaufman soon returned to offer Lawler $10,000 for joining him in a bout against Hart. Lawler walked out, grinning from ear to ear. To everyone's surprise, the King agreed to the match if Andy promised to never appear in a wrestling ring again. The bout took place on July 18, with Kaufman and Lawler against Jimmy Hart and the Assassins. Within a few minutes of the match, Andy threw white powder in the King's face. As Hart and Kaufman embraced, one of the Assassins pummeled Lawler to the mat. The four repeatedly stomped Lawler as the bell rung, and they were disqualified. A piledriver was used on Lawler by an Assassin as Hart and Kaufman each held one of his legs. The ring was cleared when Austin Idol appeared.

The following Saturday, Kaufman strutted into the TV studio wearing a crown and accompanied by Jimmy Hart and the Assassins. "I love you, Andy! The new king of professional wrestling, Andy Kaufman," Jimmy Hart exclaimed. Andy gave the Assassins the $10,000 check and then heckled Lawler and the fans. "Let me tell you something, Jerry Lawler, you were talking about how stupid I was last week. Your fans and Jerry Lawler, you're a lot stupider than I thought. You believed when I started talking about, 'Oh, I was just playing bad guy' and you were stupid enough to believe that….I think these people, they live like pigs. They don't know how to act. I am going to teach them some lessons in manners, etiquette, and hygiene." Lawler then walked out wearing a neck brace. "I'm sure that Kaufman and Hart and the Assassins are in the back somewhere seeing me here with this neck brace on after the piledrivers. Now I'm sure that they're laughing right now because you see this is what Kaufman has wanted to see for over a year now. So, Kaufman, you take a good look. I want you to look at it real hard." The real King reached up to his neck, grabbed the brace and pulled it from his neck. "I am not a stinking, little pencil-necked wimp like you and Jimmy Hart and Andy Kaufman, you see it takes more than a couple of bums like the Assassins to put me in the hospital!"

A bit later in the broadcast, the Assassins took on Mike Mashburn and David Johnson in a tag team bout with Kaufman and Hart at ringside. "Hey, here comes Lawler," said Lance Russell, interrupting Dave Brown's play-by-play. The King snuck up behind Kaufman, tapped him on the shoulder and, as he turned, threw a fireball in his face. Screams and cheers filled the studio as Kaufman fell to the floor, trying to put the fire out. The Assassins and Hart grabbed Kaufman to hold him down as he writhed in pain. Kaufman covered his face with his hands as he was carried to the back. A few minutes later, they showed Kaufman, with burn marks on his face, threatening revenge. He got his chance when Lawler feuded with future WWF star Jesse Ventura, who was being managed by Hart. The feud began in September when the King lost his southern heavyweight title. A few weeks later, he regained the belt during a match in Lexington, Kentucky. For the return match in Memphis, Lawler stipulated that Hart had to wear a chicken costume while in Ventura's corner. During the match, the chicken strutted outside the ring and flapped its wings. When referee Jerry Calhoun was knocked out and fell out of the ring, Lawler had Ventura pinned. Then the chicken entered the ring. The King rolled off Ventura and attacked the chicken before pinning Ventura again. Jimmy Hart, sans feathers, entered the ring and was wanged into the ropes. Ventura revived and raked Lawler across the face with his fist, which knocked the King to the ground. While the chicken pushed a dazed Jerry Calhoun into the ring, Ventura pinned Lawler and gained the southern belt.

Meanwhile, Kaufman filmed a series of videos that fulfilled his promise to teach Memphians "how to act." Fans wailed and gnashed their teeth when they saw these videos. To the delight of the fans, Lawler stomped the next tape into smithereens on Saturday morning TV. A year before, the fans wanted Kaufman hurt. Now they wanted him dead, at least until the next match. The week after Lawler destroyed the tape, the King announced that he was again being sued by Andy. During the broadcast, Dave Brown called Kaufman on the phone to discuss the lawsuit. He said that *Taxi* was canceled because of his burnt face, and he was very angry for Lawler smashing his videotape. During the tirade, Kaufman coughed, and while it was not noticed at the time, that spasm would have a profound effect on Memphis wrestling. Lawler picked up the phone and told him, "Any time you want to come back to Memphis, any time I can get my hands around your stinking little skinny neck, I would love it!" In reply, Kaufman dropped a bombshell. "A few weeks ago, I was in Memphis. You didn't know it, did ya? Do you remember Hart's chicken? I was dressed as Hart as a chicken, man....I stopped you from winning the southern title, you idiot!" This perfectly set up the next match, with Andy and Hart agreeing to face Lawler wearing gloves in a boxer versus wrestler match. Kaufman said he had been training with Muhammad Ali, and the tricks he learned were sure to bring him victory. Lawler stood in the middle of the ring, pointed at his chin and dared the Hollywood star to punch him. Kaufman clowned around, swung on the ropes and generally stayed away from the King while Hart stayed in the corner. "No sign of Muhammad Ali we know, this must be another Muhammad Ali," Lance Russell dryly commented. Lawler knocked Hart to the mat, and while the King was grabbing Kaufman, Hart picked up a handful of powder and accidentally threw it in Andy's face. Lawler slapped Hart back to the canvas, and then Kaufman jumped on the King's back. Bashed into the turnbuckle, Andy slid to the mat, and when Lawler moved to pick him up, Hart bawled the powder into Lawler's eyes. Writhing on the ground, Kaufman and Hart repeatedly kicked the King in the ribs and smashed his back. Hart was able to pick a dazed Lawler from the mat and hold him as Kaufman punched him back to the canvas. Lawler eventually recovered, but after a brief tangle, Hart and Kaufman used a chain on the King to win the match.

The following Saturday morning, Kaufman, Hart and the entire First Family hosted a victory party on TV. Kaufman provided color commentary with Lance Russell for a match between the First Family's Norvell Austin and Dennis Condrey against Plowboy Frazier and Art Crews. When Austin and Condrey won, Kaufman pointed a finger in Russell's face and said, "Once again we proved our point about the First Family." Later, Hart introduced the newest member of the First Family, the Russian Invader, who was scheduled to fight Lawler on Monday night. The biggest feud in the world was the Cold War between the United States and the Soviet Union, which was in a very dangerous phase during the early 1980s. Russian leadership was convinced that President Ronald Reagan was going to launch a nuclear first strike, while the United States was also suspicious due to the Soviet invasion of Afghanistan and the downing of Korean Air Lines flight 007, which killed many people, including several Americans. Two months before the Russian Invader appeared in Memphis, a Soviet satellite early-warning system malfunctioned and reported that the United States had launched nuclear missiles. Fortunately, the Russian commander on duty waited for conformation before launching their own missiles. Adding to the growing nervousness in America, the ABC television network announced the broadcast of a TV movie called *The Day After*, which would show the effects of nuclear war on the American people and was scheduled for the following night. These things were on the minds of Memphians when the Russian Invader appeared before the camera. Wearing a red mask with a hammer and sickle, the Invader showed propaganda films of a Russian military parade and told the audience, "You remember that, Sunday night! You'd better watch this movie because if you get the Russian people mad, this is what's going to happen to you!" Threatening nuclear war against the people of Memphis is never a good idea. Dressed in a red, blue and star-spangled outfit, Lawler showed up with a large bag of wheat that he put on the commentator's desk. Then he gave a lesson in American democracy:

> *Let me just tell the Russian Invader something. First of all, you're in the United States of America right now....As I've said before they're a lot of things wrong with this country but there are a lot more things right with it than there are wrong, and one of the right things is the fact that a jerk like you from Russia can come out here and have the freedom to say what you please. You can come on television in front of hundreds of thousands of*

> *people and downgrade this country, but that's because you're free to do that over here. Now, there's no way in Hades, brother, that a person like me or like Lance Russell could go to Russia and get on television and say anything derogatory about the Soviet Union because you see, you don't have those kinds of freedoms over there because there's nothing but a rotten, stinking hellhole full of a bunch of Communist jerks like you, Russian Invader. Let me tell you somethin' else. I don't think you understand, you talkin' about all these missiles and you're talking about all this stuff that you would like to and all the things that you would like to do to the people here in the United States. Well, one of the things that I said, there's some things wrong with this country and one of the things that's wrong with them is the fact that we have farmers who work day and night to grow wheat and then we turn around and sell it to jerks like you over in Russia. Millions of bushels of wheat every year we sell to the Russians, so what you don't understand is you're talking about blowing up the United States. You blow us up, idiot, and your people starve to death because you're too ignorant, you're too stupid, you're too asinine, to grow your own food! You're too busy building bombs and building missiles! I'll tell you another bit of freedom we got. We got the freedom to show a stupid movie that's comin' on like* The Day After. *I think if you ask me, I think there's some sort of Communist plot behind that because what that movie is designed to do is to make the American people afraid of the Russians. Well, let me tell you somethin', I'm not gonna watch the stinkin' movie and I don't think anybody else should watch it, because I'm not afraid of you Russian, and the Americans are not afraid of Russia and we'll kick your butt any day of the week, brother!*

A scheduled match between Lawler and Buddy Landel got underway, with Russell and Kaufman providing commentary. Talking about the King, Kaufman said, "Jerry Lawler, he's so stupid, Lance. You think he would've learned by now not to tangle with the brains of Hart and Kaufman....He's big, OK. He has a lot of brawn, but he has no brain, Lance. All he's used to doin' is plowin' the fields and farms!" When Lawler punched Landel in the face, Kaufman went ballistic. "Stop the match right now! I want that man disqualified right now....Hey, Calhoun, how much is he payin' ya?" Later, Hart jumped in the ring and punched and kicked Lawler as he was pinning Landel. The King then whaled on Hart until Landel pummeled and grabbed him. The Russian Invader then entered the ring carrying the bag of wheat. Landel held Lawler's arms as the Russian slammed the bag of wheat upside Lawler's head. Wheat went flying, and the King fell to the mat.

Hart and Landel poured wheat over Lawler's prostrate body as the Russian stuffed some of it in Lawler's mouth. "Jerry Lawler, you want to feed, you've got your way. I don't need that stinkin' wheat, the Russian people don't need that stinkin' wheat!" the Invader screamed while Kaufman did the Twist for the furious crowd. Koko Ware and the Plowboy helped revive the King, who declared, "Let me tell that stinkin' Russian Invader one thing, brother! We got a little bag and a little bit of this wheat left, and I want to tell you somethin'. I'm gonna bring this with me down to that ring this week, and there's a little bit of this wheat left in here, and I promise you, you're gonna eat this, Russian, through the other end, brother! I guarantee you that because I'm not scared of you one bit! And I'm gonna prove it to you, we're gonna see what a Russian can do to an American. I promise you, brother, you're gonna eat this one way or another!"

The next morning, Kaufman appeared on Jerry Lawler's new talk show. He didn't look well, and the cough had returned, but he was still the same old Andy. "I didn't come here to be insulted; I'll walk right out of here. I'm telling you right now I'm used to being on big shows nationwide, I'm not used to being on a little rinky-dink local show. What are you trying to be like, David Letterman with the Jerry Lawler Show....I knocked you out when I had those boxing gloves on. You just give me a pair of boxing gloves and I'll knock you out again." The boxing gloves didn't help Kaufman on Monday night. In the second round of the boxer versus wrestler bout, the King fended off Kaufman's punches to pin him to the canvas. In the title match, Lawler forced the Russian Invader to eat that wheat after crushing him in less than two minutes. However, despite the exceptional promotion, only 3,841 people attended the event.

Koko Ware, also known as Sweet Brown Sugar, was a famous Black wrestler in Memphis during the 1970s and 1980s and once helped save Jerry Lawler from the Russian Invader.

When the two men met in the ring, both knew a terrible secret. After the *Jerry Lawler Show* broadcast, Kaufman told Lawler that he had been diagnosed with lung cancer. Tabloid newspapers reported the news of Kaufman's cancer in early 1984, and during a Saturday morning broadcast, Jimmy Hart used this news as a part of his ongoing feud with Lawler. "A very close and personal friend of mine, Andy Kaufman, is dying of cancer." As the audience cheered, he said, "I know you laugh about it, you people are sick. Let me tell you what, the man who can't sleep at night is Jerry Lawler. How can Jerry Lawler go to bed at night, thinking about what he did to this man because everybody knows, five ways of cancer, baby, and the number one way of catching cancer is when you get a bruise or lump on you, man. That's cancer and he's got cancer of the brain and that's caused from that piledriver!" As tasteless as Hart's tirade was, Andy probably loved it. He died on May 16, 1984, and on the following Saturday, Lance Russell asked Lawler for comment. "I'm really the wrong person to talk to about that. You know, I didn't like Andy Kaufman and Andy Kaufman didn't like me.…It's a sad situation. I'm sorry about it, but other than that, you know, that's all I got to say." Wherever Andy Kaufman was, he must have been pleased that "Mr. Lawler" kept the storyline going. In fact, Lawler's comments did not reflect how he really felt. He would later write, "He was the neatest guy. He wasn't a weird nut, he was brilliant. He was so respectful of wrestling. He was all 'sir' this and 'yes, ma'am.' He loved everything about the squared circle, it was one of the most fun things he ever did. He was great for wrestling, and I really miss the guy."

In the early 1980s, cable television was being offered in many parts of the country, including Memphis. For the first time, viewers in the Bluff City could watch wrestling programs from Atlanta, Chicago, Nashville and other locations. According to Lawler, "In Memphis at one time, counting our show, there were about nineteen hours of wrestling on a week." Some fans stayed home to watch TV rather than go to the Coliseum. At the same time, the New York promoter Vince McMahon Jr., owner of the World Wrestling Federation, was enticing the talent out of the territories with promises of national exposure on cable TV. He created a show called *Superstars of Wrestling*, which was sold to many independent TV stations across the country, including WMKW-TV in Memphis. In May 1984, McMahon debuted *Tuesday Night Titans* on the USA cable network, which gave him a national base to steal more talent and gobble up additional territories. Memphis was next. He had already tried to destroy Jarrett with *Superstars of Wrestling*, and on June 24, 1984, he invaded the Memphis territory with a package of matches that included appearances by Andre the Giant and Hulk Hogan, who had wrestled in Memphis as Terry Boulder, in the main event against Moondog Rex. According to wrestling historian Tim Hornbaker, "Packing his cards with 'New York' stars didn't win over patrons. Memphis fans responded to emotionally charged feuds, built with a steady hand, and acted out with precision. So, the random booking of Hogan and Moondog Rex without any backstory or psychological investment was of no interest to fans." Only 1,200 people attended the WWF program, while the next night, Jarrett offered a nine-match spectacle he called "Star Wars '84." Nearly 10,000 fans watched Lawler and Austin Idol slam the Road Warriors, while Handsome Jimmy Valiant successfully defended his southern heavyweight belt against Rick Rude. The Fabulous Ones, Tommy Rich, Dutch Mantell, Eddie Gilbert and Porkchop Cash also made appearances. At the same time, Jarrett strengthened his relationship with Verne Gagne's Dallas-headquartered American Wrestling Association. For several years, Gagne had allowed his champion Nick Bockwinkel to wrestle against the King, who was a major contender for the belt. Because of their relationship with the AWA, Jarrett renamed his territory the United States Wrestling Association.

As we have seen, the NWA would not give Jerry Lawler and the USWA territory a real shot at the world championship. This is why Lawler didn't face Flair in the ring in 1982 or in 1985, when he came back to Memphis and had to settle for a match with Koko Ware. They turned to the AWA, which offered Lawler a real opportunity to capture its world heavyweight title. He wrestled champion Nick Bockwinkel several times, and this provided an opportunity for the King to finally become a world champion. Lawler got his chance on May 9, 1988, in a match against the AWA world title holder, Curt Hennig. Lawler's world heavyweight bout was of major importance in Memphis. The city proclaimed May 9 "Jerry King Lawler Day," and the local media covered every aspect of the contest. When Mayor Richard Hackett issued the proclamation, he said, "On behalf of the citizens of this community let you know that we are totally behind you, and we want to make sure that this little wimp coming into town doesn't beat our own king here in Memphis and we're going to proclaim this Monday Jerry King Lawler Day." The mayor sat at ringside during the match, joining eight thousand other citizens in watching the great Jackie Fargo referee the fight between Lawler and Hennig. Fifteen minutes into the bout, Hennig put Lawler into a Boston crab hold from which he barely escaped, but then Hennig gashed Lawler's face. With blood trickling into his eye, it looked like the King might lose his crown. But then, according to Mike Fleming of the *Commercial Appeal*, "When things looked darkest, the fans pushed new life into Lawler's tired effort. He was getting a blood transfusion from the cheers. And the match turned. Lawler sent Hennig's head into one of the corner posts and the King seized the chance. Moments later Hennig found himself pinned to the canvas with referee Jackie Fargo—and the crowd—counting him out." Lawler grabbed the belt, jumped on a corner post and held it high in the air. Cheers erupted from the crowd, whom Lawler gave credit for his victory. "But my fans came through. They helped me reach down for something extra. I've got them to thank."

Meanwhile, Vince McMahon continued to take over small territories with his talent and cable TV shows. However, the dismal performance of his product in Memphis convinced McMahon to leave Memphis alone. He did pick up a few Memphis stars, most notably Jimmy Hart and Kamala. Hart did okay in the WWF, but Kamala was exploited and cheated even though he was one of the federation's most popular performers. His matches against Hulk Hogan were legendary, and Kamala became a national figure. But as he grew older and lost his legs to diabetes, he was left with little money and fewer prospects. However, he still had millions of fans, who often supported him until his death in 2020 from complications related to COVID-19. Instead of crushing the Memphis territory, McMahon hired Jarrett and Lawler to groom new talent while also running their own territory. New wrestlers like Jarrett's son Jeff and Lawler's son Brian Christopher developed their own fan base and later moved up to the WWF. Eventually, Jarrett sold his half of the territory to Lawler, and the King was able to appear at WWF events while continuing to run Memphis. WWF stars regularly performed in the Bluff City as heels, winding the fans up by referring to Memphis as "disGraceland." Several major WWF stars—including Steve Austin, Bret Hart and Randy Savage—appeared in the Bluff City. At the same time, Memphis became the developmental territory for the WWF. However, fan interest still declined, and for some wrestlers the loss of opportunity was a devastating blow. This was especially true for Tojo Yamamoto. After the fall of Nick Gulas, Tojo returned to Memphis, where he regained much of his popularity. However, his health declined. Despondent over his career, he put a pistol to his right temple and pulled the trigger in February 1992, shocking fans and industry insiders alike. Dave Brown commented, "Tojo Yamamoto was a man who always took wrestling serious. People didn't joke about it around him. He started as a villain but became a good guy and a teacher."

Four years later, in early 1996, McMahon sent a young wrestler to Memphis named Flex Kavana. He was Dwayne Johnson, who in 1976 had lived in the Bluff City with his father, Rocky Johnson, and even briefly appeared on Saturday morning wrestling. When he arrived, the Memphis territory was in trouble. Attendance at the Coliseum had plummeted, as had the TV show's ratings, while the *Commercial Appeal* stopped reporting match results. At the Coliseum, wrestling had to compete with a hockey team for space, and stricter security measures—such as keeping the lights on, metal detectors and even frisking attendees—had alienated some longtime fans. Lawler also pointed out that nearby casinos in Tunica, Mississippi, "had a major effect on our business....Also, there are two Monday night cable wrestling shows on TV that used to not be on. A lot of people can stay home and watch wrestling for free." From 1979 to 1983, average attendance was 8,000, but in 1995–96 only 1,500 to 2,000 fans visited the Coliseum on Monday nights. These numbers could not sustain the promotion, so the USWA ended its long relationship with the Mid-South Coliseum on June 17, 1996. Billed as "The Last Blast at the Coliseum," matches included Jeff Jarrett versus Brian Christopher, Lawler against Cyberpunk and a match between the teams of Flex Kavana and Bart Sawyer and the Punisher and Tony Falk. The following Monday, USWA wrestling began a short run at the Big One flea market center, located on the outskirts of the working-class neighborhood of Frayser. Brian Christopher and Flex Kavana dominated the Big One matches, while Lawler remained the King.

Left: Brian Christopher was a popular wrestler in Memphis during the 1990s and strongly influenced Dwayne Johnson's career.

Right: Rocky Johnson's son Dwayne, seen here as Flex Kavana, learned the art of professional wrestling when he performed in Memphis during the 1990s.

Christopher was an important friend and mentor who taught Dwayne Johnson/Flex Kavana a great deal about the wrestling business and helped him become a local star. According to Lawler, "The fans got behind this kid and they really liked him a lot." In late August 1996, Kavana was called up to the WWF, which meant he had to leave Memphis in just a few days. He was too popular to simply disappear, so Lawler had to quickly decide how to tell the fans that Kavana was leaving. The two appeared on Saturday morning TV, and in true Memphis style, a match was scheduled between the King and Flex. In an interview with Dave Brown, Kavana called on Lawler to give him a shot at his world title. Lawler agreed to the bout on the condition that Kavana leave Memphis if he lost. The deal was made, and they both entered the ring. It had to be quick because they were running out of time. The show would end in a few minutes, so Lawler threw a piledriver on Flex just before the cameras turned off. Two days later, Dwayne Johnson made his WWF debut, beginning one of the greatest careers in professional wrestling. When he left, Johnson was a seasoned pro who owed much of his subsequent success to Memphis and Brian Christopher. Johnson never forgot the lessons of Memphis or his great friend. When Christopher met a tragic death in 2018, Johnson wrote:

> *RIP brother.*
>
> *Spent all week trying to process the hard loss of my good bud, Brian Christopher Lawler.*
>
> *He became a great friend the day I stepped foot in the small wrestling territory in the south known as the USWA to start my pro wrestling career.*
>
> *We rode together daily (1500 miles per week) trained together at any gym we could find, ate together at any Waffle House off the highway, wrestled together in flea markets to state fairs, shared motel rooms together, and would always dream (and talk shit) about what life would be like once we made it to the big leagues of the WWE.*
>
> *Once we both finally made it to the big leagues of the WWE, nothing changed...we still did everything together. Including having nightly Madden tournaments after our wrestling matches in our motel room and then we'd extend our competitive spirit to a rowdy game of Wiffle Ball. Imagine us acting like crazy Wiffle Ball idiots at 2am in the parking lot of the Motel 6.*
>
> *Our jaws would hurt from laughing so hard.*
>
> *Then we'd finally take our butts to bed, hit the gym in the morning, drive 200 miles to the next town to wrestle and start the night all over again.*

Jerry Lawler with his son Brian Christopher.

I'll miss these times now even more.

Hurts my heart to know how Brian decided to check out.

I never knew him to be suicidal, but I guess sometimes the pain just gets to be too much for one to take.

I'll miss you man and the times we had.

Thanks for being a great friend.

Thanks for being my boy.

My love, light, support and strength to Brian's father, Jerry Lawler and Brian's mother, Kay as well as Brian's family and friends.

He also never forgot Mempho. In 2022, he stated, "I made my bones and came up in Memphis!!! That's my city! I wrestled every Saturday morning at the channel 5 tv station and every Monday night I wrestled at the Big Top flea market." Meanwhile, Dave Brown reached his thirtieth anniversary of cohosting Championship Wrestling and decided to retire. Losing Brown was a fatal blow. Viewership was already declining, and it got worse when he left, so station programmers moved the broadcast to Midnight on Saturday nights. In September 1997, WMC-TV ceased production of the show and instead broadcast reruns. One month later, it pulled the plug entirely. After nearly fifty years, there was no local wrestling program on Memphis television. With no TV show to promote the matches, wrestling disappeared from Memphis. It happened so fast. Many old-time fans couldn't believe it. When the Coliseum closed and the TV show ended, it seemed that Memphis wrestling was over, never to return. *Commercial Appeal* columnist John Beifuss summed it up for many when he wrote, "To me, this wrestling fixation was one of the things that made Memphis distinctive, and interesting, in a weird way....I thought: Sivad is gone, Happy Hal is retired, and the WHBQuties... are probably on their third marriages; but as Humphrey Bogart might have told Ingrid Bergman if *Casablanca* had been set in Shelby County, 'We'll always have wrestling.' Wrong again. For professional wrestling...as an ongoing part of the city's (often disreputable) cultural identity is all but out for the count."

For more than a decade, Beifuss's view was correct, but something strange happened as it often does in this gritty place. In 2001, the Vancouver Grizzlies NBA team relocated to Memphis and, as a part of their own promotion, had Jerry Lawler stage wrestling matches at half time and during commercial breaks. It had been years since anyone had seen a Memphis-style wrestling match, and some basketball fans walked away remembering how things used to be. Ten years later, the documentary *Memphis Heat: The True Story of Memphis Wrasslin'* was released. Produced by Sherman Willmott, Ron Hall and Billie Worley and directed by Chris Schaffler, the film played in movie theaters in Memphis and across the old territory to widespread acclaim. It whetted the appetite of old fans while reminding them of what they had been missing. In the wake of the movie's success, several local promoters began staging wrestling matches across the city that drew hundreds of fans. These included the Real South Wrestling Federation, 901 Wrestling and Memphis Championship Wrestling, continuing to keep alive this aspect of the Bluff City's cultural identity. RSWF was founded by Jerome Williams and led by a wrestler named SoulTaker. Williams specifically created the RSWF to give Black wrestlers an opportunity to develop their skills. To that end, he gathered a talented stable of wrestlers, including Big Ace, Kevin Bless, Zach Crow, Maverick and V-Man, who carried on a brilliant feud with the SoulTaker and generated nearly as much heat as the old CWA. For example, when Big Ace met a New York wrestler who was insulting the Bluff City, he said,

Left: The Real South Wrestling Federation's SoulTaker, seen here with wrestling fan Derrick Patterson.

Below: Jerome Williams founded the RSWF to help Black wrestlers gain experience and develop their skills.

"The first thing you don't do is disrespect Memphis, Tennessee!" Then a fan screamed out, "Two things stopping you—fear and common sense." The company offered matches on Friday and Saturday nights from 2015 to 2020 in southeast Memphis and had its own cable-access TV show. In 2017, a travel writer from Australia attended the RSWF matches, which he described as "a blast, an excited crowd of adults and children really making their presence felt. From the constant taunting to the raucous lumberjack match where paying attendees were encouraged to 'interact' with the combatants as they spilled outside the ring. The audience of lumberjacks [were] each given leather straps, so the performers felt the love."

Two other local companies have also done much to revive local wrestling. Four years after *Memphis Heat* debuted, Memphian Chris Thompson went to work for an organization in Holly Springs, Mississippi, called Ultimate Championship Pro Wrestling Staff. In 2018, it started offering matches in Midtown Memphis, and the following year its name was changed to 901 Wrestling. Currently the matches are held at Black Lodge on Cleveland and are hosted by "Mr. 901," Tommy Jax, and broadcaster Kevin Cerrito. The same year that Thompson adopted the 901 Wrestling name, Dustin Starr, a veteran of the WWE's developmental training program, and his wife, Maria, founded Championship Wrestling. Offering live wrestling matches on the first Sunday afternoon of the month, the action is filmed and used in a weekly television show, which is broadcast on WMC Action News 5 Plus every Saturday at 11:00 p.m. In addition, the show is syndicated in several local markets. Taken together, these organizations have re-created Memphis wrestling, which is now being enjoyed by hundreds of people every month. It may never be as culturally significant or popular as the glory days, but it keeps an aspect of Memphis culture alive and is passing it on to the next generation. As Chris Thompson once explained, "It's in the DNA of this city and there's only a couple of things that are imbedded into Memphis: basketball, BBQ, music, and wrestling. Those things are ingrained, whether the people know it or not." As the companies were growing, Jerry Lawler continued to wrestle in Memphis, on Beale Street, at the Bluff City Fair and in front of the shuttered Coliseum.

On March 15, 2024, professional wrestling returned to downtown Memphis when the WWE's Friday Night SmackDown appeared at the FedEx Forum. The WWE had visited the Bluff City several times in the twenty-first century, but this night was special. Jerry Lawler made his first major public appearance after suffering a stroke, and Dwayne "The Rock" Johnson appeared in a Memphis ring for the first time since 1996.

901 Wrestling keeps Memphis wrestling alive and passes it on to the next generation.

Memphis Championship Wrestling, founded by Dustin and Maria Starr, produces a weekly television program on WMC Action News 5 Plus.

Dwayne "The Rock" Johnson made a triumphant return to Memphis in March 2024.

He was playing a heel with his tag team partner, Roman Reigns, against Cody Rhodes and Seth Rollins, which culminated at Wrestlemania XL. The crowd screamed and chanted when Lawler appeared, and it grew louder when Johnson entered the ring and began to speak:

> *You know usually every single week the Rock comes out here and he tortures, and he scorches every city that he's in. But, tonight, it's different. This city is different. You see, years ago when the Rock first started his wrestling career, the Rock started right here in Memphis, Tennessee. Every Saturday morning, Channel Five! Every Monday night at the Big Top flea market! Do you remember the Rock's name back then? Flex Kavana. I don't know what the hell I was thinkin', but I went for it. So, this city's a little different. So, the Rock'll say it like this. Finally, the Rock has come back home!*

No sport has ever reflected the culture of a city better than professional wrestling has for Memphis. Its defiance, creativity and violence were on display in the ring as they were in the streets. To be sure, the mat game existed throughout the United States and Europe, but by drawing on the attitudes and emotions of the people of Memphis, a unique product was developed that is still beloved by wrestling fans everywhere.

BIBLIOGRAPHY

Books

Beekman, Scott M. *Ringside: A History of Professional Wrestling in America*. Praeger, 2006.

Cosper, John. *The Original Black Panther: The Life and Legacy of Jim Mitchell*. Eat Sleep Wrestle, 2019.

Griffin, Marcus. *Fall Guys: The Barnums of Bounce*. Reilly & Lee Company, 1937.

Harris, James, and Kenny Casanova. *Kamala Speaks*. WOHW Publishing, 2015.

Hornbaker, Tim. *Death of the Territories: Expansion, Betrayal and the War that Changed Pro Wrestling Forever*. ECW Press, 2018.

———. *National Wrestling Alliance: The Untold Story of the Monopoly that Strangled Pro Wrestling*. ECW Press, 2007.

James, Mark. *Memphis Wrestling History Presents, 1977: The War for Memphis*. Self-published, 2014.

———. *Memphis Wrestling History Presents, 1982: A Legendary Year from the Golden Era*. Self-published, 2010.

Johnson, Steven, and Greg Oliver. *The Pro Wrestling Hall of Fame: The Heels*. ECW Press, 2007.

———. *The Pro Wrestling Hall of Fame: Heroes & Icons*. ECW Press, 2007.

———. *The Pro Wrestling Hall of Fame: The Storytellers*. ECW Press, 2019.

Laprade, Pat, and Dan Murphy. *Sisterhood of the Squared Circle*. ECW Press, 2017.
Lawler, Jerry. *It's Good to Be the King…Sometimes*. Pocket Books and World Wrestling Entertainment Inc., 2002.
Leen, Jeff. *The Queen of the Ring: Sex, Muscles, Diamonds, and the Making of a Legend*. Atlantic Monthly Press, 2009.
Shoemaker, David. *The Squared Circle: Life and Death and Professional Wrestling*. Gotham Books, 2013.
Zimmerman, Ken, Jr. *Gotch vs. Hackenschmidt: The Matches that Made and Destroyed Legitimate American Professional Wrestling*. Ken Zimmerman Jr. Enterprises, 2016.

Publications

Commercial Appeal.
Memphis Flyer.
Memphis Press-Scimitar.
New York Times.
Pueblo Chieftain.
TIME.

Website Sources

https://kentuckyfriedwrestling.com.
https://kenzimmermanjr.com.
http://lozintranslation.blogspot.com/2017/05/my-memphis-wrestling-experience-at.html.
https://mapleleafwrestling.blogspot.com/2018/09/stanley-stasiak-torontos-wrestling.html.
https://memphiswrestling.fandom.com.
https://prowrestling.fandom.com.
https://slamwrestling.net.
https://www.theringer.com.
https://www.wwe.com.
www.wrestlingshame.com.

YouTube Channels

Ben Affleck. https://www.youtube.com/watch?v=zxPtNUKptag.
CWAMemphis. https://www.youtube.com/watch?v=QX4kqtKegzE&list=FL4FiKowr4UQ2e7_-HsPDQHw&index=51&t=619s.
David Bayens. https://www.youtube.com/watch?v=xTndTO1tqVk&list=FL4FiKowr4UQ2e7_-HsPDQHw&index=52&t=14s.
Guerin Shea. https://www.youtube.com/watch?v=Jj8ZTdAAzFo&list=FL4FiKowr4UQ2e7_-HsPDQHw&index=36.
Kadaveri. https://www.youtube.com/watch?v=wA-Ibsc9gkA&list=FL4FiKowr4UQ2e7_-HsPDQHw&index=12.
Kentucky Fried Rasslin. https://www.youtube.com/watch?v=lhbdOj_Pm6U&list=FL4FiKowr4UQ2e7_-HsPDQHw&index=40&t=210s.
Memphis Wrestling Video Vault. https://www.youtube.com/@MemphisWrestlingVideoVault.
Popculturestu. https://www.youtube.com/@popculturestu.
RF Video Vault. https://www.youtube.com/@RFVideoVault.
Rolochoshu. https://www.youtube.com/@rolochoshu.
Saturday Night Live. https://www.youtube.com/@SaturdayNightLive.
70sTVchannel. https://www.youtube.com/watch?v=Fq9z8xflUVY&list=FL4FiKowr4UQ2e7_-HsPDQHw&index=38.
Shooter 86. https://www.youtube.com/watch?v=qdKGdacb_oU&list=FL4FiKowr4UQ2e7_-HsPDQHw&index=9.
Southerngospel. https://www.youtube.com/watch?v=TDVQ4Uqe6VY&list=FL4FiKowr4UQ2e7_-HsPDQHw&index=10.
Wcwarchive. https://www.youtube.com/watch?v=Pv9Jqxtm-_A&list=FL4FiKowr4UQ2e7_-HsPDQHw&index=32&t=30s.
WrestlingsGoldenAge. https://www.youtube.com/watch?v=mrSn2ibdgIA&list=FL4FiKowr4UQ2e7_-HsPDQHw&index=33.

SOURCES BY CHAPTER

Sources are roughly in order as they appear or are used throughout each chapter.

Chapter 1

1. Beekman, *Ringside.*
2. Shoemaker, *Squared Circle.*
3. Zimmerman, *Gotch vs. Hackenschmidt.*

4. *Commercial Appeal*, September 25, 1894; September 29, 1894; April 25, 1909; January 24, 1924; January 30, 1924; February 3, 1924; February 14, 1924; March 10, 1924; March 23, 1924; April 3, 1924; April 4, 1924, April 13, 1924; April 16, 1924; July 5, 1924; October 30, 1924; December 16, 1924; December 18, 1924; December 28, 1924; January 10, 1925; March 18, 1925; March 19, 1925; March 21, 1925; March 28, 1925.

Chapter 2

1. Shoemaker, *Squared Circle.*
2. *Commercial Appeal*, April 26, 1925; September 6, 1925; September 19, 1925: October 1, 1925; October 21, 1925; October 29, 1925; November 7, 1925; November 21, 1925; December 4, 1925; December 6, 1925; December 12, 1925; December 17, 1925; January 8, 1926; January 10, 1926; January 15, 1926; January 21, 1926; January 9, 1927; January 14, 1927; February 2, 1927; February 3, 1927; February 17, 1927; February 20, 1927; February 26, 1927; May 28, 1927; November 3, 1927; March 15, 1928; January 5, 1930.
3. *Memphis Press-Scimitar*, November 5, 1965.
4. Gary Will, "Stanley Stasiak: Toronto's Wrestling Fatality 1931," Maple Leaf Wrestling, https://mapleleafwrestling.blogspot.com.

Chapter 3

1. Johnson and Oliver, *Pro Wrestling Hall of Fame: Heroes & Icons.*
2. Johnson and Oliver, *Pro Wrestling Hall of Fame: The Heels.*
3. Leen, *Queen of the Ring.*
4. *New York Times*, June 28, 1935.
5. *Commercial Appeal*, September 8, 1931; November 24, 1931; December 6, 1931; January 7, 1932; January 29, 1932; February 14, 1932; February 28, 1932; September 25, 1932; September 27, 1932; October 6, 1932; November 29, 1932; December 6, 1932; December 23, 1932; December 30, 1932; April 8, 1933; September 20, 1934; May 8, 1935; June 29, 1935; March 20, 1939; October 16, 1940; October 17, 1940; October 18, 1940; January 19, 1943; January 25, 1943; January 30, 1943; February 1, 1943; February 13, 1943; March 14, 1943; March 16, 1943; April 25, 1943; April 27, 1943; May 30, 1943; June 11, 1943;

July 8, 1943; July 13, 1943; August 8, 1943; August 10, 1943; October 7, 1943; October 10, 1943; October 12, 1943; October 15, 1943; October 24, 1943; October 26, 1943; November 14, 1943; December 12, 1943; December 13, 1943; December 19, 1943; December 20, 1943; January 29, 1944; February 1, 1944; March 13, 1944; March 18, 1944; April 10, 1944; April 17, 1944; April 23, 1944; June 11, 1944; June 19, 1944; July 8, 1944; July 27, 1944; September 9, 1944; September 11, 1944; September 24, 1944; September 26, 1944; October 12, 1944, October 23, 1944, November 11, 1944, November 14, 1944; November 26, 1944; November 30, 1944; December 3, 1944; December 18, 1944; January 4, 1945; January 6, 1945; January 7, 1945; January 22, 1945; January 25, 1945; January 28, 1945; February 3, 1945; February 5, 1945; March 8, 1945; March 13, 1945; March 17, 1945; March 23, 1945; March 26, 1945; April 1, 1945; April 22, 1945; May 3, 1945; July 6, 1945; July 9, 1945; August 13, 1945; August 14, 1945; August 26, 1945; October 18, 1945; October 21, 1945; November 3, 1945; November 5, 1945; November 8, 1945; December 4, 1945; December 9, 1945; January 20, 1946; June 28, 1946; July 30, 1946; August 18, 1946; August 20, 1946; August 29, 1946; September 2, 1946; September 3, 1946; October 14, 1946; October 20, 1946; October 31, 1946; November 4, 1946; November 10, 1946; November 11, 1946; November 24, 1946; December 14, 1946; November 10, 1947; February 20, 1957; July 7, 1957.
6. *Time*, April 17, 1933.
7. *Pueblo Chieftain*, August 3, 2020.

Chapter 4

1. Vance Nevada, "Lou Thesz Career Record," Slam Wrestling, https://slamwrestling.net.
2. Ken Zimmerman Jr., "Wild Bill Longson Regains Title," updated June 17, 2021, https://kenzimmermanjr.com.
3. *Commercial Appeal*, January 19, 1943; January 25, 1943; January 30, 1943; February 1, 1943; February 13, 1943; March 14, 1943; March 16, 1943; April 25, 1943; April 27, 1943; May 30, 1943; June 11, 1943; July 8, 1943; July 13, 1943; August 8, 1943; August 10, 1943; October 7, 1943; October 10, 1943; October 12, 1943; October 15, 1943; October 24, 1943; October 26, 1943; November 14, 1943; December 12, 1943;

December 13, 1943; December 19, 1943; December 20, 1943; January 29, 1944; February 1, 1944; March 13, 1944; March 18, 1944; April 10, 1944; April 17, 1944; April 23, 1944; June 11, 1944; June 19, 1944; July 8, 1944; July 27, 1944; September 9, 1944; September 11, 1944; September 24, 1944; September 26, 1944; October 12, 1944, October 23, 1944, November 11, 1944, November 14, 1944; November 26, 1944; November 30, 1944; December 3, 1944; December 18, 1944; January 4, 1945; January 6, 1945; January 7, 1945; January 22, 1945; January 25, 1945; January 28, 1945; February 3, 1945; February 5, 1945; March 8, 1945; March 13, 1945; March 17, 1945; March 23, 1945; March 26, 1945; April 1, 1945; April 22, 1945; May 3, 1945; July 6, 1945; July 9, 1945; August 13, 1945; August 14, 1945; August 26, 1945; October 18, 1945; October 21, 1945; November 3, 1945; November 5, 1945; November 8, 1945; December 4, 1945; December 9, 1945; January 20, 1946; June 18, 1946; June 25, 1946; June 28, 1946; July 30, 1946; August 18, 1946; August 20, 1946; August 29, 1946; September 2, 1946; September 3, 1946; October 14, 1946; October 20, 1946; October 31, 1946; November 4, 1946; November 10, 1946; November 11, 1946; November 24, 1946; December 14, 1946; March 4, 1947; November 10, 1947; June 23, 1948; June 24, 1948; July 18, 1948; November 8, 1948; November 9, 1948; December 6, 1948; December 9, 1948; December 20, 1948; Dec 27, 1948; January 9, 1949; January 16, 1949; January 30, 1949; February 1, 1949; August 21, 1949; December 4, 1949; July 18, 1950; November 5, 1951; February 6, 1953; December 9, 1953; July 24, 1955; April 7, 1957; April 9, 1957; April 30, 1957; June 4, 1957; June 11, 1957; July 7, 1957; November 2, 1958.

Chapter 5

1. Steven Johnson, "Billy Wicks: 'Pops' Was Source of Stories, Inspiration," Slam Wrestling, https://slamwrestling.net.
2. *Commercial Appeal*, August 10, 1959; August 16, 1959; August 17, 1959; September 14, 1959; September 20, 1959; September 29, 1959; October 1, 1959; October 11, 1959; October 13, 1959; November 24, 1959; February 7, 1960; February 8, 1960; March 29, 1960; July 17, 1960 July 18, 1960; November 17, 1960; March 14, 1961; March 19, 1961; April 4, 1961; November 7, 1961 November 13, 1961 November 28, 1961; January 21, 1962; February 5, 1962; February 18, 1962; June

18, 1962; November 6, 1962; January 24, 1963; February 4, 1963; February 5, 1963; February 25, 1963; March 12, 1963; March 18, 1963; July 31, 1963; August 18, 1963; September 10, 1963; September 15, 1963; October 8, 1963; November 3, 1963; November 4, 1963; December 1, 1963; December 22, 1963; February 4, 1964; February 10, 1964; February 11, 1964; May 19, 1964; October 5, 1964; December 20, 1964; May 30, 1965; June 1, 1965; November 7, 1965; November 8, 1965; November 14, 1965; March 28, 1966; October 3, 1966; October 18, 1966; October 23, 1966; October 30, 1966; February 19, 1967; August 1, 1967; August 6, 1967; August 8, 1967; September 17, 1967; October 29, 1967; November 12, 1967; December 12, 1967; January 14, 1968; February 11, 1968; August 4, 1968; August 6, 1968; August 19, 1968; November 29, 1968; July 7, 1969; April 12, 1970; April 14, 1970; June 28, 1970; June 29, 1970; July 12, 1970; July 28, 1970; August 3, 1970; October 26, 1970; November 4, 1970; April 13, 1975.

3. *Memphis Flyer*, March 31, 2011.

Chapter 6

1. James, *Memphis Wrestling History Presents, 1977.*
2. Lawler, *It's Good to Be the King.*
3. Oliver Lee Bateman, "Jerry Jarrett Created Pro Wrestling as We Know It," The Ringer, February 16, 2023, https://www.theringer.com.
4. David Bayens, "The Original Tupelo Concession Stand Brawl '79," YouTube.
5. Pro Wrestling | Fandom, "Bill Dundee," https://prowrestling.fandom.com.
6. Scott Bowden Presents Kentucky Fried Rasslin', "Anatomy of an Angle: Robert Fuller's Last Stand in Memphis Leads to Tupelo Concession-Stand Brawl," https://kentuckyfriedwrestling.com.
7. Rolochoshu, "Buildup for Jerry Lawler vs Rocky Johnson," YouTube.
8. Guerin Shea, "Memphis Wrestling: WHBQ 1976 TV Christmas Special Part 1," YouTube.
9. Memphis Wrestling Video Vault, "Jerry Lawler, Bill Dundee—Beaten and Bruised After Concession Stand Brawl (6-16-79)," YouTube.
10. 70sTVchannel, "Memphis Studio November 1978 Jerry Lawler Jimmy Valiant Bill Dundee," YouTube.
11. *Commercial Appeal*, January 24, 1971; January 25, 1971; January 26, 1971; May 14, 1971; July 4, 1971; July 5, 1971; October 17, 1971;

January 30, 1972; February 15, 1972; April 9, 1972; April 10, 1972; June 5, 1972; August 8, 1972; December 17, 1972; January 28, 1973; February 11, 1973; March 11, 1973; March 18, 1973; March 20, 1973; March 25, 1973; April 15, 1973; April 16, 1973; April 29, 1973; June 25, 1973; June 26, 1973; July 15, 1973; July 29, 1973; July 31, 1973; August 12, 1973; September 30, 1973; November 20, 1973; December 2, 1973; March 3, 1974; March 5, 1974; March 18, 1974; March 19, 1974; March 26, 1974; April 16, 1974; April 21, 1974; April 22, 1974; June 10, 1974; June 30, 1974; July 8, 1974; July 9, 1974; July 23, 1974; July 29, 1974; August 4, 1974; August 20, 1974; September 1, 1974; September 10, 1974; October 1, 1974 October 7, 1974 October 9, 1974; October 13, 1974; December 1, 1974; December 8, 1974; January 26, 1975; February 4, 1975; July 17, 1975; July 22, 1975; December 2, 1975; December 7, 1975; December 9, 1975; December 22, 1975; March 8, 1976; June 20, 1976; June 22, 1976; July 11, 1976; July 13, 1976; July 25, 1976; August 22, 1976; November 9, 1976; November 21, 1976; November 23, 1976; November 28, 1976; December 7, 1976; December 13, 1976; March 20, 1977; September 11, 1977; September 14, 1977; September 29, 1977; January 3, 1978; November 12, 1978; November 28, 1978; May 22, 1979; July 15, 1979; July 22, 1979; July 31, 1979; August 5, 1979; August 7, 1979; August 12, 1979; August 14, 1979; August 29, 1979; June 14, 2017.

Chapter 7

1. Hornbaker, *Death of the Territories.*
2. James, *Memphis Wrestling History Presents, 1982.*
3. Lawler, *It's Good to Be the King.*
4. Memphis Wrestling Wiki, "Flex Kavana," https://memphiswrestling.fandom.com.
5. World Wrestling Entertainment, "The Last Stand of Flex Kavana: How Jerry Lawler Got the Rock Out of Memphis on 2 Days Notice," https://www.wwe.com.
6. Loz in Translation, "My Memphis Wrestling Experience at Game 6 Grizzlies and the RSWF (Real South Wrestling Federation)," May 11, 2017, http://lozintranslation.blogspot.com.
7. RF Video Vault, "Jerry Lawler on Andy Kaufman," YouTube.

8. Memphis Wrestling Video Vault, "Jerry Lawler vs Ric Flair (NWA Heavyweight Title Match) Part 2—The Hustle," YouTube.
9. Popculturestu, "The Kaufman Lawler Feud: Chapters 1–34," YouTube.
10. Ben Affleck, "Uncensored Andy Kaufman and Jerry Lawler on Letterman Full (1982)," YouTube.
11. Shooter 86, "The Debut of Kimala," YouTube.
12. Southerngospel, "Lawler 70s Promo!" YouTube.
13. Wcwarchive, "8/24/1996—USWA—The Rock (as Flex Kavana) Promo with Jerry Lawler," YouTube.
14. WrestlingsGoldenAge, "Jimmy Hart Is Done with Jerry Lawler 1980," YouTube.
15. WrestlingsGoldenAge, "Empty Arena Terry Funk vs Jerry Lawler Original Broadcast 04/25/1981, Memphis Wrestling," YouTube.
16. WrestlingsGoldenAge, "1981 Terry Funk After Empty Arena Match 05/16/81, Memphis Wrestling," YouTube.
17. *Commercial Appeal*, February 10, 1980; February 24, 1980; April 6, 1980; April 13, 1980; April 27, 1980; September 2, 1980; December 30, 1980; January 11, 1981; January 13, 1981; January 25, 1981; March 24, 1981; May 26, 1981; July 15, 1981; August 4, 1981; October 2, 1981; November 24, 1981; December 1, 1981; June 8, 1982; July 6, 1982; July 13, 1982; July 21, 1982; July 27, 1982; August 3, 1982; August 24, 1982; October 12, 1982; May 3, 1983; June 26, 1983; July 10, 1983; July 12, 1983; September 13, 1983; September 19, 1983; November 15, 1983; November 22, 1983; June 24, 1984; June 26, 1984; May 10, 1988; February 21, 1992; June 17, 1996; October 25, 1977; November 14, 1997; April 5, 2019; March 15, 2024.
18. *New York Times*, July 30, 1982.

ABOUT THE AUTHOR

G. Wayne Dowdy is the senior manager of the Memphis Public Library's history department. He holds a master's degree in history from the University of Arkansas, is a contributing writer for *Best Times* magazine and is an Eagle Scout. He is the author of eight books, including *A Brief History of Memphis*, *Enslavement in Memphis* and *On This Day in Memphis History*, which was awarded a Certificate of Merit by the Tennessee Historical Commission.

Visit us at
www.historypress.com